RECORDS OF CIVILIZATION

SOURCES AND STUDIES

Edited under the auspices of the
Department of History, Columbia University

GENERAL EDITOR: W. T. H. Jackson, Professor of German and History

Number VIII

The History of Yaballaha III

The History of Yaballaha III

NESTORIAN PATRIARCH

AND OF HIS VICAR

Bar Sauma

MONGOL AMBASSADOR TO THE FRANKISH COURTS
AT THE END OF THE THIRTEENTH CENTURY

TRANSLATED FROM THE SYRIAC
AND ANNOTATED BY

JAMES A. MONTGOMERY

1966
OCTAGON BOOKS, INC.
New York

Reprinted 1966
by special arrangement with Columbia University Press

OCTAGON BOOKS, INC.
175 FIFTH AVENUE
NEW YORK, N.Y. 10010

LIBRARY OF CONGRESS CATALOG CARD NUMBER: 66-28327

Printed in U.S.A. by
NOBLE OFFSET PRINTERS, INC.
NEW YORK 3, N. Y.

IN MEMORY OF

WILLIAM ROMAINE NEWBOLD

WHO WAS CHARACTERISTICALLY INTERESTED

AND HELPFUL IN THE BEGINNINGS

OF THIS VOLUME

EDITOR'S PREFACE

IN this little volume there has been opened up for English readers an interesting chapter in the history of the intercourse between Orient and Occident. With painstaking care in Introduction and notes Professor Montgomery has rendered the text understandable and, through bibliographical notices, has offered suggestion for further critical reading. The time is the late thirteenth century; the chief actors in the story are two travelers from far Cathay. The scene shifts rapidly all the way from Peking to the court of King Edward of "Engleterra" in Aquitaine. For Rabban Sauma, the Chinese whose diary was drawn upon for the history which is here translated, traveled quite as widely as did his contemporary, Marco Polo. And as the latter left us a narrative of his experiences in eastern lands, so here are chronicled the impressions of the first Chinese to leave a record of his visit to the West during the Middle Ages.

The oriental background of occidental culture and the contrasts between East and West furnish a fruitful field for the investigator. Scholars have for some time been at work on these problems; but the results of their labors are closed for the most part except to specialists who possess the necessary language equipment. To assist in making available to the general reader some of these materials it is planned to include in this Series translations of a number of significant works. The *History of Yaballaha III* is the first of these to see the light.

When the translation of this work was first considered, the intention was to bind with it other materials similar in content and representing the same general field of interest. After careful consideration, however, the better plan seemed to be to let this text stand alone. The publishers and the editorial committee concur in the belief that our volumes will be more useful to a wide range of readers if the works translated are offered separately, even though this may entail, as in the present case, the publication of a thin volume. Obviously from the very nature of the materials some books must consist of collections of documents or writings from various authors. But in so far as practicable the policy here laid down will be adhered to.

The burden of other work has compelled Professor Shotwell to give up active direction of this Series, which he planned and the first seven numbers of which he has edited. It is a matter of great regret that the work could not have gone forward under his most discriminating and stimulating guidance. The History Department of Columbia University has now assumed general responsibility for the editorial conduct of the Series. This is the first volume to be published under the new auspices. To those interested in the enterprise it may be useful to know that the present arrangement provides for a general editor, counselled by an advisory board, and assisted as need arises by special editors for single volumes or groups of volumes. It is our wish to continue to publish translations and studies which shall be at once readable, useful and dependable.

A. P. E.

CONTENTS

INTRODUCTION

I. THE SYRIAC DOCUMENT; EDITIONS AND DISCUSSIONS

THE names and some of the acts of the heroes of this Biography were known from Western archives long before the modern discovery and publication of our document. Papal records of the 13th century and Assemani's compilations from Oriental literatures had given the Nestorian Catholicus, or Patriarch, Yaballaha and his friend and right-hand man Bar Sauma, or Sauma, a place in history. For these personages see below, § iv. As a preliminary note on the interest of the present document it is sufficient to state that Bar Sauma was the first of Chinese birth to reach the Frankish lands and leave a record of his journey, while in general it illumines an obscure but most crucial chapter in the history of the relations between the East and the West.

A copy of a novel Syriac manuscript giving 'the History of Mar Yaballaha' came into the hands of Père Paul Bedjan, of the Chaldaean Church,[1] which he published in 1888. Subsequently other copies of apparently one and the same MS. (the original seems to have disappeared) came to light, on the basis of which Bedjan published a second edition in 1895 (Harrassowitz, Paris and Leipzig) under the title *Histoire de Mar-Jabalaha*, collating in it the readings of the several texts, and adding some other unpublished documents. A brief apparatus in Syriac of dates and biographical and geographical identifications is also given.[2] It is the text of this

---

[1] For the rise of this Uniate body (*i.e.*, one in communion with the See of Rome) out of the Nestorian Church, see Assemani, *Bibliotheca orientalis*, iii, pt. 2, c. 8, and for some of its subsequent history Badger, *The Nestorians and their Rituals*, 1852, 1, 145, *et seq.*

[2] One of these MSS. is in the British Museum (Or. 3636). Mr. J. Leveen, of the Oriental Department of the Museum, kindly examined it for me in one point where serious doubt had been raised, but there was no variation in reading. An earlier announcement of the document appeared in a communication by Prof. H. H. Hall

edition that the present translation follows. The subject has been vastly enriched by a French translation given by J. B. Chabot, 'Histoire de Mar Jabalaha III,' in the *Revue de l'Orient Latin*, 1 (1893), 567–610; 2 (1894), 73–143, 235–304, with ample notes and at the end chronological and dynastic tables, followed by several Appendices, *ib.* 566–638, presenting for the first time and with full treatment the pertinent Western archives, etc. As this Catholic review appears to be difficult of access (I have been able to find a copy only in the New York Public Library), the translation by the eminent Syriast, not to say the Syriac original, has been generally ignored by subsequent English histories and bibliographies bearing on the relations between East and West in the Middle Ages.[3] Hence the present partial translation may be justified for drawing attention afresh and in English dress for the first time to a very remarkable document. I may add that for the most part my annotations as well as translation are independent of Chabot.[4]

in the *Proceedings* of the American Oriental Society, Oct., 1886, pp. iv–vii, with much more exact detail as to the provenance of the MS. and its copies, one of which came through the American Protestant Mission at Urmia into Dr. Hall's hands, and he gives a digest of its contents. He notes that a translation of the document into the modern Syriac dialect appeared in issues of the Syriac journal of the Mission, 1885–86. It thus appears that the discovery was actually made by the American missionaries. I have made inquiries in various possible quarters for the present location of Dr. Hall's MS., but have been unable to trace it. Dr. Hall also published in the same *Proceedings*, 1889, p. clxxxi, an additional note bearing upon Bedjan's first edition, and animadverting upon the latter's statements as to the discovery of the MS.

[3] I note as exceptions the second edition of Yule, *Cathay and the Way Thither*, to which the editor (himself a French gentleman), Cordier, has added an abstract of the Biography drawn from Chabot, vol. 1 (1915), 119–121; T. F. Carter, *Invention of Printing*, 1925, 127, citing Cordier; and the Syrian–English scholar Mingana in a recent article (see § iii, note 2).

[4] For critiques of Bedjan's work the following may be cited: T. Nöldeke, *Literarisches Centralblatt*, 1889, 842–844; T. J. Lamy, *Bull. de l'Acad. Belge*, 17, 223–243; R. Duval, *Journal asiatique*, ser. viii, 13, 313–354; H. Hilgenfeld, *Textkritische Bemerkungen zur Tesh'ita de Mar Yaballaha*, Jena Thesis, 1894 (of small substantial value). See bibliography in Baumstark, *Gesch. d. syrischen Literatur*, 326.

II. THE MONGOLS AND THEIR RELATIONS WITH THE WEST

THE middle of the 13th century witnessed the final bankruptcy of the Crusades. The doom of the great enthusiasm was registered in Saladin's capture of Jerusalem in 1187. There followed several so-called Crusades, among which only Emperor Frederick II's brief recovery of Jerusalem gave any ray of hope. But a third party now entered into the lists where Christians and Muslims had been engaged. These were the wild and for long invincible Mongols out of Eastern Asia. Their dominion was established by Jenghis Khan (b. 1155, d. 1227). He left to his family and people an empire which ruled from Northern China to the Caspian. These were pagan barbarians of the Shamanistic stage of religion, who in their first overflows defied at once all established religion and civilization. The Muslims who met their blows in South-western Asia were equally their victims along with the Christians whom they exterminated in Russia. Under Jenghis' son Ogdai (1227–41) the Mongols conquered Korea and their hordes overran Eastern Europe, beyond Russia into Bulgaria, Hungary, Poland, as far as Thuringia. As Loewe remarks, "Had not the death of Ogdai recalled Batu and his generals, there is little doubt but that Paris and Rome would have shared the fate of Moscow and Kiev."

This disturbance of the ancient balances in Asia and Europe facilitated, however, opportunities for enterprises which, had they succeeded, would have absolutely changed the complexion of Asia and of Christendom. In the first place a new door was opened into the heart of Asia; travellers, traders, ambassadors, missionaries found their way in comparative security through the breadth of the Mongol lands; overland routes *via* Russia and Asia Minor around the Caspian were now practicable, while the Muslims rendered difficult the passages to the East by Egypt and Syria.

3

And Pope Innocent IV (1243–54) conceived the masterly idea of converting the Mongols to Christianity and so uniting them with the Christian West in a final Crusade against the Saracens. With the following document contributing to the demonstration, this bold idea was more than a will-o'-the-wisp; it proved to be practical politics until nearly the end of the century. For this narrative tells the story of a joint mission from the King of the Western Mongols and the Patriarch of the Nestorian Church in 1287 invoking the aid of Christian Europe in a campaign against the Saracens for the recovery of the Holy City Jerusalem.[1]

[1] The monumental work on the Mongols is that by H. H. Howorth, *History of the Mongols*, London, 1876–88. H. M. J. Loewe contributes the chapter on the subject in the *Cambridge Medieval History*, vol. 4 (1923), c. 20. A readable but undocumented history was presented by Jeremiah Curtin, *The Mongols*, Boston, 1908. Yule-Cordier, *Cathay*, gives a review of the history and still more fully Cordier in his *Histoire de la Chine*, 1920. Of particular value for many detailed points are G. Devéria, 'Notes d'épigraphie mongole-chinoise,' in *Journal asiatique*, series ix, vol. 8, 94–128, 395–443, and E. Bretschneider, *Mediæval Researches from Eastern Asiatic Sources*, 2 vols., London, 1910, both drawing fully from the Far-Oriental materials. The latter has an excellent map showing the ancient routes across Asia in the 13th century. W. E. Soothill, *China and the West*, Oxford, 1925, gives an admirable review of the general subject. But these authorities confine themselves in the end to the Chinese development of the Mongol empire of Kublai Khan and his successors, and so ignore the Western Mongols, or Ilkhans, with whom our history is concerned. Their particular history has received no recent treatment, while much of the original material, in Persian and Arabic, still remains inaccessible for practical purposes.

The Oriental sources appear to have been first used by B. d'Herbelot in his *Bibliothèque orientale*, Paris, 1697, Hague, 1777–79. Subsequent histories inclusive of the Ilkhans are d'Ohsson, *Histoire des Mongols*, Hague, 1834–35, Amsterdam, 1852, and J. von Hammer-Purgstall, *Geschichte der Ilchane*, Darmstadt, 1842. Another elder authority, still useful for its summing-up of all the then-known materials bearing on the political and religious relations between the Mongols and the West, is L. Mosheim, *Historia Tartarorum ecclesiastica*, Helmstadt, 1741 (ignored in the bibliographies— a copy was kindly put at my disposal by my friend, the late Prof. Wm. R. Newbold); one-half of this valuable work is devoted to the texts of the Papal and other archives bearing on the relations with the Mongols. A most useful work is L. Bréhier, *L'Église et l'Orient au Moyen Âge*, 1921, with a capital survey of the politics and diplomacy for our century; see especially, cc. 7–10. The pertinent articles in the *Encyclopædia of Islam* may be consulted; and for the dynasty of the Ilkhans see Lane Poole, *Mohammadan Dynasties*, 217, et seq. Yule's *Marco Polo* is an invaluable reference book; I have been able to use only the first edition, 1871. For further bibliography, bearing especially on the Nestorian missions in the Far East, the contacts of Inner Asia with Latin Christendom and the Chinese sources, see § iii, note 2.

The chief Christian-Syrian authority is Bar Hebraeus (properly Gregory Abu l'Faraj), 1225–1286, with his 'Secular History,' Syriac text edited by Bedjan, *Chronicon*

These at once pious and politic plans of Western Christendom resulted in several missions to the Mongols. The most famous of these were that of the Franciscans, John de Plano Carpini and Benedict the Pole, commissioned by Innocent IV in 1245, and that of William Rubruquis (of Rubruck) sent by the saintly Louis IX of France in 1252 while he was in the Holy Land.[2] Another commission, of Dominicans, Ascelinus and others, sent by the Pope, proceeded in 1245 to the Western Mongols in Persia. The arrogant demands of these embassies were met with equal bluffness on part of the Khans, but they brought home the first direct information of the heart of the Mongol empire.[3]

syriacum, Paris, 1890, and translated into Latin by P. J. Bruns, Chron. syr., Lpzg., 1789; and his 'Church History,' ed. by Abbeloos and Lamy, Chronicon ecclesiasticum, Loewen, 1872–77. A continuator has carried on his work to a later date, so that it is made contemporary to our Biography. Further, there are the invaluable Syriac materials collected by Assemani in his Bibliotheca orientalis, 1717 seq., with large excerpts from Bar Hebraeus. Note particularly his section in vol. iii, pt. 2, 101 et seq., 'Nestorianorum status sub Mongolis.' One of his chief authorities is the Arabic Chronicle of the Patriarchs by 'Amr, an extensive section from which is given below at end of § iv. The writings of the Armenian kings Haithon (or Hethum) I and II constitute other contemporary sources. The 'Journey' of the former king to the Great Khan in 1254–55 is given by Bretschneider, Mediæval Researches, 1, 164–172. (For this Armenian material see the Bibliography to Loewe's chapter in the Camb. Med. Hist.) The principal Muslim authority is Fazlullah Rashíd, whose lifetime (1247–1318) synchronizes with the subject of our Biography. The sumptuous text and translation of his Persian work, the Collection of Histories, by E. M. Quatremère, Histoire des Mongols de la Perse, 1836 (a copy in the New York Public Library), only goes through Hulagu's reign, and so does not help us. The E. J. W. Gibb Memorial has begun publishing the text, with introduction; two volumes have appeared. On this author see Yule–Cordier, Cathay, 3, 107–112.

For geographical descriptions of the lands of the Western Mongols see Guy Le Strange, Mesopotamia and Persia under the Mongols in the 14th Century, A.D. (Asiatic Society Monographs, v), 1903, with excellent map, abstracted from the Nuzlat al-qulub of Hamdullah Mustaufi, the geographical portion of which he has since published at length in the Gibb Series, 1919; also in general his Lands of the Eastern Caliphate, 1905, and Baghdad during the Abbasid Dynasty, 1900 and 1924. For the geography and description of the sacred places of the Nestorians see Assemani, l. c. c. 14; Georg Hoffmann, 'Auszüge aus syrischen Akten persischer Märtyrer,' 1880, in Abhandlungen f. d. Kunde des Morgenlandes, vii, no. 3.

[2] The travels of these two commissions have been published by the Hakluyt Society: The Journey of William of Rubruck, in translation by W. W. Rockhill, 1900, and The Texts and Versions of John de Plano Carpini and William de Rubruquis, by C. R. Beazley, 1903. Mangu's letter of response to Louis is given by Mosheim, App. xiv.

[3] For a review of these missions see especially Mosheim, pp. 43 et seq. (fully documented), also Bréhier, pp. 220 et seq., Yule–Cordier, Cathay, 1, 154 et seq., and Cordier,

The third in succession and direct descent from Jenghis was Mangu, whose court it was Rubruquis visited. His brother Hulagu, who ruled over the West in his name, annihilated the Abbaside Caliphate at Baghdad (1258), practically destroying that city and massacring its inhabitants, but exempting the Christians, saving them from the common ruin by confining them to one quarter, as Bar Hebræus records. His further campaign through Syria towards Egypt was stayed by a decisive defeat at Ain Jalût, under the Biblical Gilboa, by the Mamluk sovereign Kutuz in 1260. (The latter was soon after assassinated and succeeded by his lieutenant Baibars, who with his successors destroyed the last vestiges of Crusade power in Syria.) This critical setback may have particularly opened the eyes of the Mongols to the advantages of an alliance with the Christian Franks. Upon Mangu's death in 1259 his other brother, the famous Kublai Khan, succeeded as emperor of all the Mongols, but Hulagu was retained as his faithful lieutenant in the West. With the latter there was established a dependent dynasty of the Western Mongols, and it is with his descendants that our document is concerned. He was succeeded by his son Abaga, 1265–1281.

We may note here another contributing factor to these relations with the West, the presence of Christian queens in the Mongol courts, where the queen-mothers held a dominant position. Indeed reports reached the West that many of the Khans themselves were Christians. Hulagu and his brothers the two Khans Mangu and Kublai, and another, Arikbuga, had a Christian mother, a woman of great force of character.[4] Hulagu had a Christian wife, Dakuz Kathon (*Kathon*='lady'), who had been a wife of his father, and whom he had taken to himself after Mongolian fashion. She played an important part in favoring the Christians against the Muslims,[5] and through her influence Hulagu had a Christian

Histoire de la Chine, at length in vol. 2, cc. 22–24. Assemani, iii, 2, 116, first collates the Papal documents bearing on Arghon's embassy to the West. He learned from them only that our Bar Sauma took part in that mission, and so had no knowledge of our Biography.

[4] See Howorth, 1, 188; Soothill, *China and the West*, 43; Bar Hebræus, *Chron. syr.* 488=Bruns, p. 533, in Assemani, iii, pt. 2, 103. Her name in the Syriac is Sarkothani Bagi; other known forms of it are Sarkuti Bagi, Siurkusteni. I suppose that most correct is Pelliot's transcription of it, Soyorghachtani-bagi (*T'oung Pao*, 15, 628).

[5] Bar Hebræus, *ib.* 491=Bruns, p. 536, Assemani, p. 108. Also there is a citation

church attached to his camp, which possessed the right of announcing its services by sounding the wooden *semantra*, or gongs (*cf.* p.
87*).[6] She died in the same year with her husband, and the
Syriac chronicler records "the grief of the whole Christian world
over the departure of these two great lights and champions of the
Christian religion." The young king Abaga went further by making a royal marriage alliance with a Christian court. He gained
for wife Maria, a bastard daughter of Michael VIII Palæologos,
who in 1261 had recovered Constantinople from the Latin Empire.
The lady was convoyed to him, according to Bar Hebræus, by the
Patriarch of Antioch.[7] This is 'the Great Queen Qotai Kathon,'
who in 1279 saved a number of Christians from massacre at the
hands of the Muslims.[8] Her influence lasted for long, as Bar
Hebræus informs us:[9] "Since Baidu [a nephew and a successor of
Abaga, in 1295] had long been familiar with Despina [*i.e.*, Greek
despoina, 'mistress'][10] daughter of the Greek emperor, whom
Abaga had married, he was favorably inclined to the Christians.
For some years she had the privilege of a church and the ringing
of gongs in the Camp." This must be the lady who as Tawos
Kathon appears as the founder of the Church in the Camp in our
narrative, p. 91*. There are probable references to the same lady
at pp. 43*, 47*. Thus these Christian queens played their part
in religious politics, as our document also shows. Abaga's son,
King Arghon, had a Christian wife, to whom Pope Nicholas IV
addressed a formal letter.[11] Towards the end of his reign he had
a son baptized, p. 88*, and p. 58* speaks of 'some of the children
of the King and Queen' as baptized.

King Abaga sent several embassies to the West: in 1267 to

in Assemani, ii, 251, referring to the 'believing Queen Dakuz Kathon,' who helped
Yaballaha's predecessor Denha to the Patriarchate against certain cabals.

[6] See Bréhier, p. 219. These ladies were of the Kerait Tartars, who were con-
verted according to Bar Hebraeus in the 11th century; see Pelliot, *ib.*

[7] *Chron. syr.*, 521 = Bruns, p. 567. *Cf.* Assemani, p. 110, citing Du Cange (*Famil.
Aug. Byzant.*, 235); also Mosheim, p. 64, for the Byzantine sources. Du Cange's
source indicates that she was espoused to Hulagu, but that the latter having died
upon her arrival she was married to Abaga.

[8] *Chron. syr.*, 539 = Bruns, p. 587.

[9] *Ib.* 595 = Bruns, p. 642.

[10] Also known as Bina, Assemani, p. 110.

[11] *V. inf.* He had two Christian wives in fact.

Clement IV, to which response was made in the name of the Pope and the King of Navarre; in 1274, when the delegates were presented to the Council at Lyons by Gregory X, where the union of East and West was solemnly, but fatuously proclaimed, and when the Mongol ambassadors were baptized;[12] in 1277 to John XXI, whose successor Nicholas III responded with a large embassy bearing letters to Abaga and Kublai.[13]

Abaga was succeeded by a brother Tangodor, 1281, who went over to Islam, the first of the dynasty to do so, assuming the good Muslim name Ahmad. His brief reign of two years was terminated by the rebellion of Abaga's son Arghon, in which he lost his life, and the nephew gained the throne, 1284. See pp. 43* et seq. and notes. Arghon's whole interest was pro-Christian. He later announced (in his Mongol letter, inf. note 16) that he would become a Christian if God vouchsafed to him to take Jerusalem. His mind appears early in the fact that in the year after his accession he sent an embassy to Honorius IV, bespeaking a joint enterprise against the Saracens. The letter presented in his name, composed in amusingly and amazingly barbarous Latin, was preserved in the Papal archives.[14] He notes that his own mother was a Christian (was it Maria Palæologa, named above?), refers to the perversion of his brother 'Ahmet,' and then calls for a common war against the Saracens and especially the land of Egypt. This letter is specifically addressed to the Pope, the King of the Franks, and King Charles, i.e., Charles I of Anjou.

In 1287 King Arghon sent another embassy to the Papal court. This was undertaken in conjunction with Yaballaha Patriarch of the Nestorians, of the traditional See of Seleucia-Ctesiphon, actually located at Baghdad. The embassy consisted of Bar Sauma, a Visitator or Archdeacon, holding episcopal rank (' a bishop

---

[12] Bréhier, p. 240.

[13] For these embassies see the literature cited note 3 and also note 1. For the Papal archives in question, which are given in extenso by Mosheim and Chabot (a summary of Chabot's results in Yule–Cordier, Cathay, 1, 166, note), I have consulted Raynald's continuation of Baronius, Annales ecclesiasticæ, vol. xiii (1694), xiv (1692). Certain English archives are cited from Rymer, Foedera, 1727 et seq. Chabot uses at times other and fuller materials, with variant texts. See Raynald, xiv, sub anno 1267, nos. 70, 71 = Mosheim, App. xix, for the Papal response, which informs the Mongol that he in conjunction with the kings of France and Navarre was agitating a crusade.

[14] Raynald, sub anno 1285, no. 79 = Mosheim, App. xxv.

in parts of the Orient' he is termed in the Papal letters), and three others whose names are preserved for us in the Papal archives.[15] These were Sabadinus, whom the Pope addressed in a personal letter as a Christian, Thomas de Anfusis (from his name doubtless a Christian), and the interpreter Uguetus, the two latter having accompanied the embassy of 1285. The presence of these experienced travellers explains how the embassy was able to interpret its mission to the strange lands it visited. With the names of these two Christian dignitaries, the Patriarch Yaballaha and Bar Sauma (or Sauma), his faithful friend and lieutenant, our particular story begins, for the Syriac document concerns their life and fortunes.

We may briefly resume the succeeding negotiations between Mongols and Franks at this period. Chabot records (2, 592 *et seq.*; 616 *et seq.*) two subsequent embassies from Arghon to the West. The first of these, 1289–90, was conducted by a Genoese, one Buscarel, and we possess, in addition to the responses written to Arghon (p. 595) and Kublai Khan (p. 597), the original Tartar letter presented by the embassy, which Chabot gives with a translation.[16] The final embassy was conducted by a Christian convert Chagan, *ib.* 616 *et seq.* Thus Arghon sent four embassies to the West in his 7–8 years of reign. Further, there is to be noted the mission (unrecorded by Chabot) of John de Monte Corvino to the court of Arghon, 1290–91. After John's first trip to the East (to Constantinople) and his return to Rome in 1289, Pope Nicholas IV sent him East again with letters to Arghon, Kublai and other potentates. He remained in Tabriz in Arghon's jurisdiction till 1291, and then proceeded to Peking, where he established the Latin Church.[17] Bar Hebræus notes briefly that in this reign frequent embassies were coming to Arghon from the Pope and then refers to the mission of 'the monk Rabban Bar Sauma the Uighurite,' who entered into a league with the Pope for the extirpation of the Arabs.[18] For subsequent correspondence between

---

[15] See the full citation of these letters in § iv.

[16] Chabot, 2, 601 *et seq.* This and another letter from King Uljaitu, a son and successor of Arghon, to Philip IV, 1305, are preserved in the French Archives. These letters have been treated by A. Rémusat, *Mémoires de l' Académie des Inscriptions*, vols. 7, 8, and in a monograph by I. J. Schmidt, St. Petersburg, 1824.

[17] See Yule–Cordier's Introduction to the Letters of this John, *Cathay*, 3, 3 *et seq.*

[18] *Chron. syr.* 579 *et seq.* = Bruns, p. 627, cited by Assemani, p. 116.

East and West we may note, after Chabot, 2, 613 *et seq.*, a letter of Yaballaha to Benedict IV,[19] and some letters dispatched by Edward I of England to the East; one of these is a letter to Arghon, of date 1290, and another to Yaballaha, March 12, 1303.[20] Also there is preserved a letter from Edward II to 'the Emperor of the Tartars on the Extirpation of the Mahometan Heresy,'[21] *i.e.*, Uljaitu, successor of Ghazan. This correspondence and also a reference to Edward I in a letter of Honorius IV [22] indicate that king's particular interest in the proposed Crusade; and this interest, which dated back to his own experience as a Crusader in Palestine when Crown-Prince (1271), may well have been augmented by Sauma's embassy, which visited him at his court in Aquitaine, pp. 72* *et seq.*[23] Mosheim also records two commissions sent by Boniface VIII to the Ilkhan court, one composed of Franciscans in 1296, the other of Dominicans in 1298, but with what results we are ignorant.[24]

For the political relations between the Western Mongols and Christendom after Arghon's death and through the first decade of the 14th century see Bréhier, pp. 264–268. Bréhier's remarks on

[19] See Raynald, *sub anno* 1304, no. 23.

[20] Chabot, 2, 614; 613 *et seq.* The former is given in Turner's paper, cited below note 23, at p. 48, note 6.

[21] Rymer, iii, 34; *cf.* Yule, *Marco Polo*, 2, 409.

[22] Raynald, *sub anno* 1291, no. 32 = Mosheim, App. xxxv.

[23] See particularly a paper by T. Hudson Turner, 'Unpublished Notices of the Times of Edward I, especially of his Relations with the Moghul Sovereigns of Persia,' *Archæological Journal* (of the British Archæological Institute), 8 (1851), 45–51. The writer cites Lingard to the effect that upon Edward's arrival at Acre " Abagha, the Tartar Khan of Persia, proposed to him an offensive alliance against the common enemy of the Moguls and Christians." Rymer, ii, 428, 498, gives a Papal letter of introduction for Buscarel's embassy to Edward, of October, 1289, and two further letters of same import, of December, 1290. And Buscarel's embassy was actually received and entertained in London, for thirteen days from January 5, 1290, according to the Royal Wardrobe Account; see Turner, p. 48. Also F. Macler, in *Camb. Med. History*, 4, 176, states, without citation, that one of Abaga's commissions to the West (*v. sup.*) in 1276 announced their arrival to Edward. Altogether the English king appears to have been most keen in these negotiations. For similar relations with the French kings Turner, note 3, registers the work by A. Rémusat, *Mémoires sur les relations politiques des princes chrétiens et particulièrement des rois de France avec les empéreurs mongols*, Paris, 1822.

[24] Mosheim, p. 87. The Papal diploma of the first commission he repeats in App. xli from Wadding, *Annales ordinis Minorum*, v, 345. The letters for the later commission he gives in App. xlii from Raynald, *sub anno* 1299, no. 39.

the pregnant possibilities of a Crusade at that time in conjunction with the Mongols against the Saracens, particularly Egypt, are worth citing (pp. 258 *et seq.*). The combined action, he says, of the Christians and the Mongols would have rendered Egypt's condition most critical and the success of the Crusade certain. The fermenting plans of a Crusade were possessed with a very practical spirit and with ideas which witness to openmindedness and to a real knowledge of the Oriental situation. Christianity never had had so clear a sense of the place it held in the world; no such moment had ever appeared for directing a decisive attack against the Muslim world. But the high and statesmanlike plans remained speculations. And we may add, it was at the end of this century that militant Christendom missed the greatest opportunity in its history.

But if the immediate cause of Christianity failed, the Mongols played an enormous part in the history of civilization. With their empire stretching in the 13th century from the Yellow Sea to the Persian Gulf, the Black Sea and the Volga, they were the intermediaries of exchange between East and West to an extent never before developed, and not repeated again until the discovery of the all-sea route to China, while indeed the land route has never since been reestablished. There was give-and-take in the exchange of the natural products of the two extremes of the continent, and in the contact of the arts the Mongols gave the West gunpowder and the printed book.

This record of the fraternal relations between East and West would not be complete without reference to Marco Polo, whose journey on his return home brought him to the Ilkhan court, where indeed he may have personally met Yaballaha. The conditions of this visit were quite romantic. King Arghon's wife, a princess of Cathay had died, leaving her express desire that her husband should wed none but one of her own kin. Arghon accordingly dispatched a 'very gallant' embassy to Kublai Khan on this quest. The latter responded, found 'a maiden of 17, a very beautiful and charming person,' and as the Messrs. Polo were now desirous of returning home, the Khan put the lady in their charge. The party made the great journey from China around by the Indian Ocean and the Persian Gulf; but on their arrival they found that Arghon had died. Evidently nothing loth, a son of his, 'Casan,' took the lady as his bride. This prince subsequently ascended the throne; see pp. 98* *et seq.*[25] Another connection between our Christian pilgrims and Polo is found in the largely identical route the two parties took across the heart of Asia. We can follow the road of the former, pp. 18* *et seq.*, *via* Tangut, the Desert of Lob, Khotan, Kashgar, to Tus in Khorasan. Polo's party traversed the same road in the opposite direction, i, cc. 33–45: Kashgar, Khotan, the Great Desert, the province of Tangut and its capital 'Camphichu,' possibly the city of Tangut of the Biography. And as Peking was the home of one of the two monks, so it was the objective of Polo. Now Polo spent three years in traversing Asia until he reached Peking in 1275 (Yule, p. l.), and Yaballaha was ordained Patriarch in 1281 in his 37th year (p. 38*), so that it is at least possible that the parties passed one another *en route*.

SUPPLEMENTARY NOTE.—In Prof. T. F. Carter's recently published work, *The Invention of Printing in China and its Spread Westward*, Columbia University Press, 1925, I find the following interesting information. Recently in the Vatican archives a whole series of letters from the Persian Ilkhans has been found; and also two letters from the Patriarch Yaballaha III to the Pope, dated 1302 and 1304, with Arabic text and Uighur seals. A list of these documents has been published by M. Paul Pelliot in an article, 'Les Mongols et la Papauté,' *Revue de l'Orient Chrétien*, 1922–23 (series iii, vol. 3), pp. 3–30; and a full treatment of these documents is promised by M. Pelliot in forthcoming numbers of that journal.

GENEALOGIES AND SUCCESSIONS OF THE GREAT KHANS AND THE ILKHANS

The following tables are taken from Lane-Poole, *Mohammadan Dynasties*, 201–221 (based on Howorth's *Mongols*). Lane-Poole's orthography, from which the Syriac forms in the Biography vary, is retained here.

[25] See Yule, *Marco Polo*, the Prologue of the narrative, cc. 17, 18, and *cf.* Yule's Introduction, pp. lii *et seq.* The travellers started in 1292, and the voyage lasted for two years or more. Polo arrived home in 1295. Book iv, cc. 1 *et seq.*, contains a lot of romantic material on the Ilkhan history, which was doubtless acquired by Polo during his stay at that court. Marco's narrative also serves to illustrate many an item in our Biography, as the notes will show.

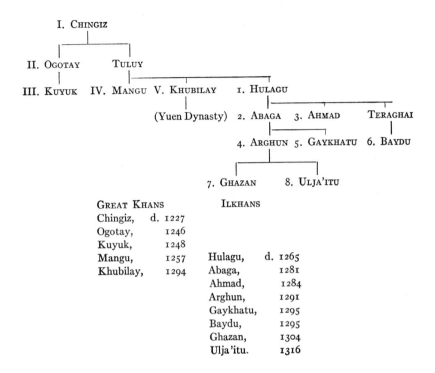

I. CHINGIZ

II. OGOTAY   TULUY

III. KUYUK   IV. MANGU V. KHUBILAY   1. HULAGU

(Yuen Dynasty)   2. ABAGA   3. AHMAD   TERAGHAI

4. ARGHUN 5. GAYKHATU   6. BAYDU

7. GHAZAN   8. ULJA'ITU

GREAT KHANS		ILKHANS	
Chingiz,	d. 1227		
Ogotay,	1246		
Kuyuk,	1248		
Mangu,	1257	Hulagu,	d. 1265
Khubilay,	1294	Abaga,	1281
		Ahmad,	1284
		Arghun,	1291
		Gaykhatu,	1295
		Baydu,	1295
		Ghazan,	1304
		Ulja'itu.	1316

III. THE ORIENTAL (NESTORIAN) CHURCH [1]

THESE Christian personalities engaged in a political mission to the West from a Mongol king open up yet another vista in the Mediaeval history of Asia, that of a potent Asiatic Christian Church, whose influence upon the barbarian Mongols proved itself at least for a time of immense importance. The Nestorian schism was caused by the anathema laid upon the doctrines of the Antiochene theologian Nestorius at the Council of Ephesus in 431. Banned by the Empire his followers more and more found refuge in the Persian (Sassanian) Empire, where they created a truly Oriental Church; indeed the division between them and the West was ultimately as much political as ecclesiastical, for they were the Christians of Persia, which was involved in mortal warfare with the Roman (Greek) Empire. Consequently this Church faced Eastward and became actually what it called itself, the Oriental Church. Its missions pushed in that direction with noble zeal and devotion. It early planted Christianity in India, where this Church survives in the Malabar Christians.[2] How early the mis-

[1] It is an unfortunate bit of nomenclature that the term 'Eastern' is generally applied by Western Christendom to the Greek Church, with or without thought of the equally ancient Churches in Asia and Africa which are not in communion with the Greek Church. The official title of the Greek Church does indeed include the epithet *anatolikē*, 'Eastern,' but this in contrast to the West. In matter of fact the Greek Church holds geographically a central position, and 'Oriental' by any proper use of the term should be used of the distinctly Asiatic Churches. The Nestorian Church calls itself 'Oriental,' and from its history as the dominant Communion in Asia more than other deserves that title. To call them Nestorians is no more correct officially than the Protestant term for Latin Catholics as Papists, or the Catholic names for Protestants as Lutherans, Calvinists, etc. It is hardly necessary to remark that there is another Syriac-speaking Church, that of the Western Monophysite Jacobites.

[2] According to tradition the Church in India was founded by the Apostle Thomas. For recent defences of the genuineness of this tradition see A. Medlycott, *India and the Apostle Thomas, an Inquiry with a Critical Analysis of the Acta Thomae*, London, 1905; and J. N. Farquhar, 'The Apostle Thomas in North India,' *Bulletin* of the John Rylands Library, 1926, 80-111. For the earliest collection of materials on the Oriental expansion of the Church see Assemani, iii, pt. 2, c. 9, with treatment of the missions

14

sionaries reached China is not known. Arnobius (3d century) in his *Apology*, ii, 12, vouches for Christians among the Chinese: "Enumerari possunt atque in usum computationis uenire ea quae in India gesta sunt, apud Seres [the Chinese], Persas et Medos." However the Chinese control in those early days reached towards the borders of Persia. See in general the Preliminary Essay in Yule-Cordier.[3] The Nestorian monument with an inscription in Chinese and Syriac at Singan-fu (as the place is commonly called) in the province of Shen-si, is the earliest local record of Christian missions in China. The stone was erected, according to its dating, in 781 A.D., and records the bringing of the Faith into that capital of the empire in 636. Subsequent records prove the continued zeal and success of the Nestorians, and it looked fair for a time that Christianity might become the religion of the empire.[4]

in India, Tartary and China. An excellent survey of the sources is presented by A. Mingana, 'The Early Spread of Christianity in Central Asia and the Far East: A New Document,' *Bulletin* of the John Rylands Library, 1926, 296–367 (with text and translation of a newly discovered Syriac document bearing on the subject). Sachau, 'Zur Ausbreitung des Christentums,' *Abhandlungen* of the Berlin Academy, 1919, gives a survey of the ecclesiastical spread and administration of the Church in the East. The amazing archæological discoveries in Central Asia and the fast-developing science of Sinology have opened up vast fields of unexpected knowledge. The following notable essays written from those points of view have been consulted: G. Devéria, a series of articles entitled 'Notes d'épigraphie mongole-chinoise,' in *Journal asiatique*, series ix, vol. 8, 1896 (with a chronology of the relations of China with the West between 1221 and 1371, largely based on Chinese sources); P. Pelliot, 'Chrétiens d'Asie centrale et d'Extrême Orient,' in the Sinological journal (Leiden), *T'oung Pao*, 15 (1914), 623–644; H. Cordier, 'Le christianisme en Chine et en Asie centrale sous les Mongols,' *ib.* 18 (1917), 49–113; the summary view in Yule-Cordier, *Cathay*, 1, 110 *et seq.*; and for geography C. E. Bonin, 'Note sur les anciennes Chrétientés nestoriennes de l'Asie centrale,' *Journ. as.*, ser. ix, vol. 15, 584–592. I have not seen the work by W. Barthold (tr. R. Stübe), *Zur Geschichte des Christentums in Mittelasien bis zur mongolischen Eroberung*, Tübingen, 1901. See also the bibliography in § ii, note 1.

[3] Withal there was a far closer connection between the East and West of Asia at the beginning of the era than is generally realized; the trade routes were open, unmolested by the later hordes and wars of religion. The Syriac writer Bardaisan, c. 200 A.D., is well informed on the morals and manners of the Chinese, while the recent discoveries of the spread of Manichæism through the centre into the far East of Asia illustrate the progress of Nestorian Christianity. For these discoveries and their results see Alfaric, *Les écritures manichéennes*, 1918-1919, and F. C. Burkitt, *Religion of the Manichees*, 1925.

[4] We now possess what appears to be a definitive work on this inscription, the volume by Prof. P. Y. Saeki (of the Waseda University, Tokyo), *The Nestorian*

A romantic development of the fame of these conversions to the Faith in Inner Asia was the marvellous story of Prester (Presbyter) John and his Christian kingdom, which became one of the objects of research for travellers and learned men, and lent hope of political support to the great plan of the West to evangelize Asia.[5]

The outburst of the Mongols in the 12th century, with all its horrors and devastations, resulted actually in establishing a wide dominion extending for the length of Asia and in providing for those who had the *entrée* a security of passage over the continent. This was proved by the European missions already referred to, and by the classic journey of Marco Polo to the court of Kublai Khan (1269–1295). As Loewe remarks (p. 629): "Apart from mere negative results, the growth of the Mongol power was responsible for other developments in the East. The first and foremost of these was the unification of Asia. This must not be interpreted in the modern sense of unity or homogeneity. The Mongol government secured tranquillity within its vast borders. The roads were open and a traveller could, as things went, count upon a safe journey. . . . There was complete religious toleration, and it is only a superficial judgment that will ascribe this to spiritual indifference on the part of the Mongols."

Furthermore the Mongol hordes were exposed to the fate of every barbarian element intruding into a higher civilization, the fascination of its religion. The Mongols in their wide sweep over the world were confronted with four such religions, Confucianism,

Monument in China, published by the S. P. C. K., London, 1916. He has worked out some most interesting identifications with Chinese history, further proving the effects of Christianity upon the Chinese. Saeki adopts the spelling Hsi-an-fu (p. 2), modern Hsingan, for the city, which for five centuries was the capital of China (p. 4); the stone was located at the imperial city. At Hankow in the south there survive the remains of a handsome Nestorian Church, observed by Polo, ii, c. 76, *cf.* Yule's note, p. 157. The last reference to Nestorians in China is a statement by the Jesuit missionary Ricci, who in 1608 found a miserable remnant of them in Sin-gan-fu.

[5] On Prester John see the materials in Assemani, pp. 488 *et seq.*; Mosheim, pp. 29 *et seq.*; Yule, *Marco Polo*, 1, 205 *et seq.*; Cordier, *T'oung Pao*, 18, 52 *et seq.*; and the brief statement by Mingana, *Early Spread of Christianity*, 309 (citing Cordier's edition of Yule, Marco Polo, 1, 237). The tradition of the conversion of a whole Turkish tribe, related by Bar Hebraeus for the year 1007 (*Chron. eccl.*, iii, 279), is more than paralleled by the facts we now possess about the conversion of large groups of the peoples of Central Asia, like the Ongut and Alain Tartar tribes, along with their kings; see the works cited above.

Buddhism, Christianity, Islam—not to name the retiring wave of Manichæanism, which had planted itself among many of the elder Turkish tribes. The first three were rooted in the heart of Asia, were non-militant, and were not viewed with political hostility. Islam on the other hand sturdily bore the brunt of their attack on Southwestern Asia, and so was long reckoned as an enemy-religion. In the end the Eastern Mongols adopted the Chinese religionism; for some generations in the West they dallied with Christianity. This was due to the subtle and powerful spiritual influences of Nestorian Christianity, abetted by motives of policy in joining hands with Christian Europe against the common foe in Islam. But in the end, by the close of the 13th century, the die was cast, and the Mongols adopted officially the faith of the Arabian Prophet. It may be left to the historian of politics and religion to determine why and how. Confession must be made, on whatever account, of the actual failure of the Nestorian Church in Asia. But in the latter half of the 13th century it appears that that Church was on the point of evangelizing the Western Mongols. And the following document is a first-hand monument of this history, for it gives unique inside information for just that critical period. Had Arghon, following in the track of statesman-like popes, won over the West to his plan of a Crusade against the Mamluk power, the centre of Islam's resistance, he might have become the Constantine of his Mongols. His grand idea perished, unsupported, and despite the favorable attitude towards the Christians of his immediate successors, Gaykhatu, Baidu, Ghazan, Islam triumphed. We may speculate on the change in the world's history which would have been involved, had the Western Mongols turned Christian.[6]

[6] Amazing reports were indeed brought back to the West of the actual conversion of Mongol potentates, e.g., of Kublai Khan. But these reports were fallaciously based on the inquisitive interest or even favorable inclination of the Khans in regard to Christianity, especially in despite of the hostile Muslim power in Egypt. None appears to have been more favorably inclined to Christianity than the Ilkhan Arghon, but he made his conversion conditional on the capture of Jerusalem; and our intimate document shows that none of the Ilkhans whom it presents was an actual Christian. But it is interesting to note that this favorable attitude towards Christianity went so far that not only did these Khans attend the Christian services, marry Christian wives and even have some of their children baptized, but also that coins of Arghon and his father Abaga bear Christian legends; see *Journ. as.*, ser. ix, 7 (1896), 514; 8 (1896), 334.

IV. THE PERSONAGES AND FACTS OF THE BIOGRAPHY AS KNOWN FROM EXTERNAL SOURCES

FOR the two heroes of our document we possess the following external information long in possession of Western archives.

In his list of the Nestorian Patriarchs, vol. ii, Assemani records Yaballaha (p. 456) for Era Sel. 1593–1629 (=A.D. 1281–1317), gives the names of the consecrating bishops, and notes the several removals of his body from its first resting-place in Baghdad.

The Continuator of the Jacobite historian Bar Hebræus gives a brief note upon Yaballaha in his *Chron. eccl.*, § ii, p. 451 (cited by Assemani, iii, pt. 2, 113, and by Bedjan, p. vi). The passage tells how two 'Yaghurite'[1] monks had come from China on pilgrimage to Jerusalem; being prevented by the difficulties of travel due to the Mamluk control of Syria-Palestine, they turned aside to Baghdad. Here the Patriarch Denha made one of them Metropolitan of China, he taking the accession-name Yaballaha. Upon

---

[1] 'Yaghurite'='Uighur.' The Uighurs were a notable Turkish race of Western Mongolia in the oasis of Turfan, a focus of Nestorian Christianity and Manichæanism, and a chief civilizing agency among the Mongols, to whom they contributed their script of Syriac-Manichæan origin. (For the exact origin of this script see the writer's *Aramaic Incantation Texts from Nippur*, Philadelphia, 1913, pp. 32 *et seq.*, and plate xl.) For this people see Howorth, i, 21 *et seq.*, Bretschneider, *Mediæval Researches*, i, 236–263; and for the recent remarkable discoveries of Uighur-Manichæan (also Christian) remains, first made by Grünwedel and von Le Coq, Yule-Cordier, *Cathay*, i, 62 *et seq.;* for the Syriac sources Assemani, pp. 467 *et seq.* Bretschneider notes, p. 262, that in the Syriac sources the name denotes Turks of Eastern Cathay. Also the Arabic biographical notice of Yaballaha by Amr, given at the end of this section, speaks of him as a Turk. And thus, although Bar Sauma was born in Peking (p. 4*) and Yaballaha was a native of a place not far distant from that capital (p. 9*), the two may not have been Chinese by race. However, the story of Bar Sauma's youth has a distinctly Chinese flavor. For the distribution of Christianity among the Asiatic races the following remark by Pelliot is pertinent, *T'oung Pao*, 15, 643: "Ce christianisme extrême-oriental du XIIIe et du XIVe siècle était surtout le christianisme de populations non-chinoises; c'était la religion d'Alains, de Turcs, peut-être un peu de vrais Mongols."

Denha's death a certain emir Ashmot,[2] a fellow-countryman of the pilgrims, suggested to King Abaga, then in his last year, that it were good policy to appoint to the Patriarchate one who was a Mongol in race and tongue, and on the King's order the election was consummated. This datum is additional to the account of the election given in the Biography, pp. 33* *et seq.*; the interest of the King and the politics involved in the election of a Mongol patriarch are to be noted. The chronicler adds that "Yaballaha, although deficient in education and Syriac letters, was nevertheless a man of fine nature and commendable piety, and he showed great affection to us and our people," *i.e.*, the Jacobites.

For the mission to the West in which Yaballaha's vicar engaged, and which was undertaken at the behest of the Mongol King Arghon, 1287–88, we have only the testimony of the Western archives, with one exception, in Bar Hebræus.[3] This person is the other 'Yaghurite,' whose name in the Biography always appears as Sauma with the prefixed title Rabban ('our master'), but in Bar Hebræus, Amr, Arghon's diploma and the Papal archives as Bar Sauma ('Bersauma'), the original form of his name.[4] The Papal archives contain copies of four letters written in response to this mission by Pope Nicholas IV. Two of these are addressed to Arghon, one to his Christian wife, 'Charissimæ in Christo filiæ Tuctani reginæ Tartarorum,' and one to Sabadinus Archaon,[5] a Christian member of the embassy.[6] Also a contemporary letter from the Pope to Kublai Khan informs that potentate of

---

[2] This Ashmot also appears in a judicial process against a Persian dignitary, whose condemnation he effects, Bar Hebræus, *Chron. syr.*, 542 = Bruns, p. 591; and also in the Arabic biography cited below. See also p. 25*, note 29; p. 41*.

[3] See § ii, note 18.

[4] 'Bar Sauma' = 'son of fasting,' after a common type of Syriac name; the constant title 'Rabban' has dislodged the first element. In one place in the Papal letters the title 'Roban' is given Bar Sauma. The name is common, *e.g.*, that of a notable ecclesiastic in the 5th century, and also of an Arabic poet in the *Aghâni*.

[5] 'Archaon' is accepted by Chabot on Klaproth's authority as meaning 'Christian.' A long discussion of the term by Yule, *M. Polo*, 1, 254 *et seq.*, reaches the conclusion that the word has some racial significance. But Devéria, pp. 397, 436 *et. seq.*, shows that the Chinese use of the word means Christian priests; he derives it from Greek ἄρχων, which passed over into Syriac and Persian.

[6] See Raynald; for the two letters to the king, *sub anno* 1288, no. 36, and the letter to the queen *ibid.*; the letter to Sabadinus no. 35. They are given by Mosheim, App. xxvi, xxvii, xxviii, xxxi.

the mission of 'certi nuncii' from 'the Magnificent King Prince Arghon,' which he has had the pleasure of receiving.[7] It is of value to give this documentation as at least a testimony to the historical character of the Biography. It may be noted here that Bar Sauma had reached Naples by June 24, 1287 (see note to p. 54*), and that he was still in Europe, at Rome, on the First Sunday after Easter, 1288 (p. 82*), Easter falling March 28.

We now possess in addition to the above sources a full biography of Yaballaha, from the Arabic Chronicle of the Patriarchs by 'Amr ibn Matta of the 14th century, published by H. Gismondi.[8] An extensive and lively notice is given of Yaballaha, and we have to suppose that the narrative was written soon after his death, as the list of the Patriarchs terminates with his death. It runs parallel to our Biography, but the two are manifestly independent. Rabban Bar Sauma is well known, but nothing is said of his mission to the West. As a contemporary document, with its picture of the personality and the prestige of the Patriarch and his relations with the Ilkhan court, it is worthy of reproduction. I give the pertinent parts of it, as follows.

THE ARABIC BIOGRAPHY OF YABALLAHA III

THIS Father was a young man of handsome figure. He wore a round beard. He occupied the patriarchal see until he reached an extreme age.

[7] Raynald, *sub anno* 1289, no. 62=Mosheim, App. xxxii.

[8] *Amri et Slibæ de patriarchis Nestorianorum commentaria*, 2 vols., Rome, 1896, 1899. The section in question is to be found in the second volume, at the end, respectively, of the Arabic text and the Latin translation. Amr was one of Assemani's chief authorities on the Patriarchal history. The MSS. Gismondi has edited are in the Vatican. For the Chronicle series of which this work is a part see the brief description by Baumstark, *Gesch. d. syr. Literatur*, 5 *et seq.* My attention to this biographical notice of Yaballaha was first directed by an obscurely entitled article by the one-time French consul at Mosul, M. Siouffi, 'Notice sur un patriarche nestorien,' in *Journ. asiatique*, ser. vii, vol. 17 (1891), 89-96. The editor makes public an Arabic MS. which had fallen into his hands, one badly dilapidated and defective, often illegible. He cites from it in full in French translation the biography of Mar Yaballaha III, and indicates its other contents, which prove it to be a form of Amr's Chronicle, as indeed appears from comparison with Gismondi's text. I have found no further reference to Siouffi's publication, which is thus initial, and of what has become of his MS. there appears to be no record. I am indebted to the Library of Columbia University for the loan of Gismondi's volumes.

He was Turk by birth and came from the country of Cathay;
he had left the service of the Khan in order to travel. The reason
of his arrival in this country was that he might visit the Holy City
[Jerusalem]. The Khan had committed to him some vestments
which he was ordered to baptize in the Jordan and to put in contact
with the tomb of the Lord Christ.

When he arrived at the Camp [9] and communicated his firmans
and orders which he had to the Great Sultan Abaka Khan, the
latter responded thus: "The road is not safe. You have a great
fame and your repute is widespread in all lands; that is why I
fear for your safety."

He was accompanied by his master and teacher who had
instructed him and rounded his education and who had initiated
him into the religious life. This teacher was called Rabban Bar
Sauma. He possessed regular features, a tall and fine figure and
an agreeable manner. He answered the Sultan: "If the condition
is as you say, we will go and present our homage to our Father and
Patriarch the Catholicus Mar Denha; we will gain his benediction
and afterwards return home."

He betook himself to him [the Patriarch] at Baghdad, where he
stayed for long. They went up to the Camp, whence, after consecrating him archbishop of Tangut, the Patriarch sent him back
to his country. Yaballaha, who was already chosen by the Highest
for the Patriarchate, found no route by which to return to his
flock. Accordingly he returned to Arbel and took residence in the
convent of Mar Sabrisho Bakuka.

One of the most reverend of the monks of this convent said to
him one day: "Thy stay here can be of no use; rise and go to
Baghdad, for God has chosen thee to rule His Church. Upon
thy arrival the Catholicus will be dead, and the Patriarchate will
be entrusted to thee." The name of the monk who spoke these
words to him was Rabban Sulâqâ.

Yaballaha made his preparations and went to Baghdad [where
he arrived] on Monday, the first day of the Dominical Fast.[10]

---

[9] Siouffi transliterates the word as Ardava, which I took to represent Ardabil,
one of the capital cities of the Ilkhans in Adharbaijan; but Gismondi has the pointed
Arabic al-'urdû, Hindustani-Persian for 'camp.' For the term see p. 15*, note 3, etc.

[10] Denha died Feb. 24; see p. 38*, note 19.

He found the Catholicus dead and the people praying by his body in the church. As soon as he was buried, Yaballaha went up on the *bêma*, where he shed hot tears. He kissed the lips of the deceased and received from him the Patriarchate, in accordance with what had been said to him.[11] The assembly of the Faithful rejoiced at his coming, and they all cried: "Behold our Catholicus and Patriarch!" Some days later the conclave of the Fathers as well as the citizens of Baghdad testified their allegiance to him, declaring by a document bearing their signatures that they had elected him.

He betook himself forthwith to the Honored Camp and presented himself to Abaka Khan. This prince rejoiced, and invested him with a magnificent robe of honor. He provided him with equipment beyond count, and sent him back accompanied by a great prince named Ashmat, who was of the family of the Khan.[12]

The new Patriarch arrived at Baghdad covered with honors and respect, and after making his preparations, went down to the monastery of Madâ'in. The day of his arrival was a holy day; it was the Saturday before the first Sunday of the Entrance.[13]

[There follows a list of the ordaining bishops, twenty-one in number. It is identical with the list given by Assemani; see p. 38*, note 19.]

He was consecrated Patriarch at Madâ'in the First Sunday of the Consecration of the Church; and he wore a pale-colored *bîrôn*. The consecration took place 1593 Seleucide Era. On that day he ordained a large number of deacons, and when he left the altar to ascend the chair, a great quantity of small pieces of gold and silver were showered upon him. No one could get into the temple, the crowd was so great. Then he went down to the monastery of the Apostle Mar Mari, where he was received according to customary usage.[14] After this he went up to Baghdad, where he had a similar reception.

[11] This physical contact with the deceased is naïvely represented as a means of transferring the succession.

[12] For this royal reception see p. 35*. For Ashmat see above, note 2.

[13] Another name for the season of the Kuddashta; the dating is the same as in our Biography; see p. 38*. For Madâ'in = Seleucia-Ctesiphon and the patriarchal church of Kôkê see p. 23*, note 19, p. 37*.

[14] For this locality see p. 23*, note 19.

This prelate reached a degree of glory and power which none had hitherto had, to the extent that the Mongol Kings, the Khans and their children, uncovered the head and kneeled before him.[15] His orders were executed in all the kingdoms of the East. In his time the Christians were very much honored and very powerful; but toward the end of his life they were in great disfavor. Then began again the payment by them of the capitation tax and the harassments which have continued to our day. The Patriarch built a great monastery near the city of Maragha, and in his time the new church and the patriarchal palace were taken.[16]

[There follows the notice of the Patriarch's death, with its exact dating in the Christian and Arabic eras, and his burial; *cf.* the similar account at the end of our Biography.]

[15] This is a unique statement of the honor paid by the Ilkhans to the Patriarch; compare the royal act of courtesy recorded p. 87*.

[16] A full account of the building of this church is given p. 92*. The last sentence refers to the later despoliation of these buildings.

V. THE STORY OF BAR SAUMA'S MISSION TO THE WEST

THE present translator has limited his task to the first half of the Biography (99 out of 205 printed pages), namely, the portion that gives the early history of the two Chinese monks, their pilgrimage to Western Asia, their settlement and ecclesiastical elevation there, and Sauma's mission to the West, terminating with the latter's death in 1293 and the accession of King Ghazan in 1295. The last section of the translation tells of the storms that were brewing for the Christians. What follows is a sad story of the vicissitudes they suffered from their Muslim enemies, the persecutions amounting to local desperate wars at Marágha and Arbéla and elsewhere, even despite the occasional favor of the kings, who seemed powerless to help them much. The story terminates with the death of Yaballaha in 1317. The Biography was written by one who was in part a witness of these turbulent events. What hope there had been of the Nestorian evangelization of the Mongols was dissipated forever; they became the devoted followers of the Arabian Prophet.[1]

Apart from the œcumenical importance of the Biography with its vista into the international ranges of politics and religion in the 13th century, there is its interest as a 'Traveller's Tale,' brought back by an observant Oriental from the strange lands to which

---

[1] In the last century Kurdish hostility had driven a large part of the Nestorian Christians out of Turkey into the more benevolent lands of Persia to the East. In the Great War and afterwards their position here became intolerable, whence they trekked by a long circuitous route to Mosul. Probably all left in Turkish territory have been annihilated. They live in and about Mosul, about 40,000 souls according to Mingana, in great economic distress under the protection of the British Mandate, and an 'Assyrian' battalion is one of the mainstays of the British forces in Iraq. The young Patriarch, who holds his office by hereditary right, is now at school in England. The political head of the Church is his aunt, the Lady Surma, 'Regent of the Assyrian Nation,' who in 1926 paid a visit to America on behalf of her afflicted people. The only other fragment of the ancient Church is on the Malabar coast of India; see G. M. Rae, *The Syrian Church in India*, 1892. This Malabar Church is now in communion with the Jacobite Syriac Church.

he was commissioned. Himself a Chinese from Cambalu-Peking and the contemporary of Marco Polo, he deserves our remembrance as an Oriental antitype of the great Venetian. The story of the mission begins with p. 47*. Sauma appears to have kept a diary; this was written in Persian and was much abbreviated by the biographer, as the latter states, p. 85*. The first person of the diarist occasionally survives in the narrative, pp. 71*, 73*, 74*.

Sauma's particular interest was in the religious life of the West which he found so akin to his own Christianity, although on a far more magnificent scale. He carefully records the 'marvels' of the great churches he saw, very particularly their relics.[2] His description of the rites of Holy Week and Easter at Rome, at which he was an honored guest, has its historical interest. I have endeavored in my notes to the text to check up these references from current sources, but with no attempt to exhaust the antiquarian details.[3] Of course it must be borne in mind that he describes buildings which have largely disappeared or else been most radically altered, and so his descriptions are all the more interesting. In Paris he saw the creations of St. Louis, Sainte Chapelle and St. Denis in their pristine beauty.

Other things than religious also struck the traveller's eye. He notes the eruption of Aetna (p. 53*), and the perpetual summer on the Riviera (p. 74*). In Naples he witnessed from a convent roof soon after his arrival a sanguinary battle in the streets, and marvels at the custom of the Franks that they kill none but the contestants (p. 54*). At Genoa he notes the democratic constitution of the city (p. 67*). A unique datum, I understand, is his figure for the number of students at the University of Paris, which he gives as 30,000; his accompanying very exact description of the studies at the University indicates his learned interest (p. 70*).[4] The message the King of England gave him

[2] For the Nestorian devotion to relics see Assemani, pp. 365–368, with the opening statement: "Reliquias sanctorum apud Nestorianos in summa veneratione haberi infinitis testimoniis probari potest."

[3] I have referred in particular to Marucchi, *Basiliques et églises de Rome*, 1909, being vol. 3 of his *Éléments de l'archéologie chrétienne*; A. C. J. Hare, *Walks in Rome*, ed. 18, 1909, and the indispensable Baedeker.

[4] The Nestorians were distinguished for their learning and great schools; see Assemani, pp. 919–951.

(p. 73*) for King Arghon is characteristic of the Frankish mind, as also a pertinent statement of the difference between the Mediæval East and West: to tell him that in the land of the Franks there are not two creeds but only one, that which confesses Jesus Christ, and that they are all Christians. Finally we may notice his interview with the Cardinals on his first visit to Rome in the Papal interregnum, in which he doughtily maintained his own confession (pp. 56* *et seq.*); we may wonder how the discussion was carried on by those men of different tongues. But Bar Sauma was a polyglot, *cf.* p. 48*.

For convenience of reference to the original, the pagination of Bedjan's Syriac text in his second edition is given in the text of the translation with asterisked figures in brackets.

THE HISTORY OF MAR YABALLAHA

THE HISTORY OF MAR YABALLAHA

[THE STORY OF RABBAN SAUMA]

[3*] THERE was a certain Believer,[1] a freeman, who feared God, rich in the things of the world and those of natural character, and well known in family and race, whose name was Sheban the Visitator.[2] He dwelt in the city Khan-balig, [4*] the royal city of the Country of the East.[3] He was legally united to a wife

[1] The Oriental name, as in the New Testament, for Christians.

[2] The Visitator (*sâ'ôrâ*) or Periodeutes (this Greek word was also carried over into Syriac), was generally a chorepiscopus, with itinerant commission, an office like that of Archdeacon, which word also appears in the Syriac. See Assemani, iii, pt. 2, 826 *et seq.* The title *sachora* is given to Bar Sauma in the Mongol letter to King Arghon, see Int., § ii, note 16. Chabot doubts whether the Visitator was a bishop, but in addition to Assemani's testimony to the office, three of the Papal letters refer to Sauma as 'episcopus in partibus orientis.' Chabot's objection is based on the principle that bishops cannot be married, as was Sauma's father, and later Sauma himself, p. 5*. Priests, deacons, even monks, might be married, but not bishops, according to Badger, 2, c. 36; however, Assemani in his treatment of the subject notes, p. 327, some regulations whereby bishops losing their wives were allowed to remarry. The point is further clinched by the fact that the Chinese Inscription refers by name to certain sons of chorepiscopi; see Saeki, p. 114, who thinks that this may have been an indulgence to Chinese ideas. But there was apparently wide liberty in the matter in that Church. To be sure, Sauma is always called 'Rabban,' which according to Assemani, p. 799, is used of presbyters, as 'Rabba,' is of bishops; but the title may have become personal in his case.

[3] The Cambalu (other travellers more correctly Cambaluc, Cambaleg, etc.) of Polo, *i.e.*, Peking; see his description of that great capital of Kublai Khan, bk. ii, cc. 11 *et seq.* The name means Khan's City (Yule, 1, 333), or rather Khan's Camp (Loewe, p. 640). Other references to the Christians of Peking known to me are as follows. There are the numerous lists of the Metropolitancies of the Nestorian Church, always including that of Chanbalek, *e.g.*, Assemani, ii, 458, iii, pt. 2, 630, while in the latter volume, p. 523, he gives a considerable list of known Metropolitans of China, to which are to be added those named in our Biography, George and Nestorios, pp. 7*, 11*. Polo refers to '5000 Christian, Saracen and Cathayan astrologers' operating in that city, c. 33. John of Monte Corvino, who in the '90's of that century established the Latin Church in Peking, reports in the opening of his First Letter that 'the Nestorians have grown so powerful in those parts that they will not allow a Christian of another rite to have ever so small a chapel, or to publish any

named Kyamtha. As time went on and they had no heir, they committed themselves in prayer and supplication to God, that He would not deprive them of one to continue the family and to be a comforter to them. He in His grace and love accepted their prayer and was compassionate to them; for He is wont to receive the entreaty of the broken-hearted and to listen to the cry of those who entreat and pray. 'Everyone who asks receives, and who prays finds, and who knocks to him it is opened' [Matt. 7-8]— when one speaks with a confidence based on a true hope. For [divine] visitation is made to both orders, men and women, when with set purpose they offer request. For there was Hannah the wife of Elkanah, who was not restrained when she prayed with fixed purpose [1 Sam. 1]; and the wife of Manoah, who was not repelled when she received the angel readily to her chamber, and he breathed the Spirit into the womb of the woman, and she bore [5*] a son.[4] Then they called him Sauma.[5] And they rejoiced with great joy and they gave joy to their neighbors and kin.

And when they had brought him up in a commendable rearing to the age that was fit for teaching, they committed him to a suitable teacher, and they schooled him zealously under him in the Doctrines of the Church. And they betrothed him. And he was qualified for the order of Priesthood, and he was numbered among the Clergy, and he became Verger in the church of the aforesaid city. And he behaved himself with all modesty and humility. And he was zealous for possession of the things that are excellent [Phil. 1:9], and he strove for the conduct of life that belongs to the things to come, until he was twenty years old. And there was kindled in his heart the light of God and it burnt up the under-brush of the sinful and purified his bright soul from uncleanness and all impurity. For he loved more than aught else the love of his Lord, and was not willing when he took hold of the plough to look back. The shadow of the world he rejected at once and forthwith denied its delights; [6*] foods that putrefy [?] he deemed

doctrines different from their own'; see Yule-Cordier, *Cathay*, 3, 46. A report upon them is also given by a Latin emissary in 1329; see Cordier, *T'oung Pao*, 18, 61.

[4] A midrashic development of the story of the birth of Samson, Jud. 13. I cannot trace it otherwise in Jewish or Syriac literature. The Arabic *Tales of the Prophets* gives a similar story for the birth of Jesus.

[5] See Int., § iv, note 4.

as though they had not come into existence, and intoxicating liquor he despised.

When his parents perceived this, great affliction overtook them and vehement sorrow beset them, lest their only son should be separated from them. So they rose up with bruised heart and implored him and offered him worldly promises: "Why, dear son, dost thou desire separation from us? Why dost thou delight in our vexation? Why is our sorrow sweet to thee? Consider, with whom will our property remain? Think, who will be our heir? Deliberate, who will acquire our labors? How can it please thee that our seed and name be extinguished? Why does thy purpose move to the effect that strangers shall inherit us?" And when they persuaded him with tears like these and afflicted him with their cries and with such talk, he obeyed them on the surface and lived with them in the body, but not of his will. And when he had served them, his parents of the body, for three years, he still [7*] did not desist from his labor and strove faithfully in his laborious course.

And so when they saw that their counsel was profitless and their word was reckoned as naught in comparison with the love of the Christ, they allowed his desire. Then he divided all his possessions, *i.e.*, his clothes and articles, among the poor. And he assumed the garb of monkhood, and he was shorn by the holy and devout Father, Mar [6] Georgis the Metropolitan. And he began to work in the vineyard of his Lord with his hope set on the Kingdom to come and with confidence in the goodly possession in heaven, that he would receive the full wage of the penny [Matt. 20:1 *et seq.*]. He took a cell apart and shut himself up in it for seven years. And afterwards he resolved to go away from men and to exercise himself in the mountains in an isolated place, so that he might satisfy himself with the monastic life. And he departed and went a day's journey from their city and chose a lodgment there; and he found [8*] in that mountain a place in a cave and by its side a spring of water. And he dwelt there with satisfaction and gave acknowledgment to his Lord, who made him equal for these things. And at last the news went forth in that

---

[6] '*Mâr*'='mi-lord' is the common title of religious respect, given both to the Saints and to dignitaries of the Church; sometimes below it is translated 'Reverend.'

country, and people began to gather to him to hear his word.
And honor was attributed to him by all.

[THE STORY OF MAR YABALLAHA]

In the foreknowledge of God is everything known, and the
purposes of all men, whether of the Right or the Left,[1] before
they are formed in the womb are revealed to Him. Therefore
according to them [*i.e.*, the purposes] he elects and justifies, and
because of them he torments and troubles. To Moses it was said:
'Behold, I have made thee a god to Pharaoh' [Exod. 7:1]—the
election of him because of his [fore]known good will; [9*] and also
the hardheartedness of Pharaoh, for even before he was it was
known that he was hardhearted, so that he was rejected. And
so He said to Jeremiah: 'Before I formed thee in the belly I knew
thee, and before thou camest out of the womb I consecrated thee and
made thee a prophet to the nations' [Jer. 1:5]. And Paul said,
'Did God cast off His people' whom 'He knew from the beginning?'
[Rom. 11:1, 2], *i.e.*, because of their fair good will and pure purposes. Now of the election some marks are shown in the person
chosen, and there rise in him rays of light which indicate that he
is worthy of the grace. He who is illuminated recognizes them,
but the unskilled does not know them. Since the elect person
was one in whose case there is the concern of an exalted life, we
must tell the method of his election and confirm this as comple-
mentary to his will.

There was in the city Koshang [2] in the Country of the East [10*]
a faithful and righteous man, pure and spotless, who served God
in His Church faithfully and behaved himself in His laws with
distinction, by name Bainiel, an Archdeacon. And he had four
sons, the youngest of whom was called Markos.[3] This one was

---

[1] An ancient Gnostic distinction between the good and the bad; also *cf.* Matt.
25: 31 *et seq.*

[2] Chabot suggests identification with Polo's Cacian-fu (bk. ii, c. 60), according
to Yule and others Hokian-fu (Hokien), 120 miles south of Peking. But Pelliot,
T'oung Pao, 15, pp. 632, 634, identifies it with Tong-chen, a town in the Ongut country
(Odoric's Tozan or Cozan), west of Peking. The Christian princes of the region are
met with in the narrative below, p. 15*.

[3] Born 1244; *v. inf.* p. 38*; accordingly in the reign of Khan Ogotay.

instructed in the Doctrines of the Church beyond all his brothers. And the guests [4] reproved him with such words, and it appeared to them that they were arguing with a pillar rather than with a reasonable man. And despite his being repressed in many ways he did not turn from his way, nor did his purpose forego its quest, but he fixed his aim and went off to Rabban Sauma by a fifteen days' journey with great fatigue. And when he greeted Rabban Sauma, the latter rejoiced in him and received him with gladness.

And after he had refreshed himself, he [Sauma] asked him: "My son, whence comest thou? And how has it occurred to thee to come to this mountain? [11*] And of what city is thy family? And who is thy father and what thy pedigree?" And he replied: "I am son of Bainiel the Archdeacon, of Koshang, and I am called Markos." And he said to him: "What is thy reason that with such labor and fatigue thou hast come to me?" And he answered him: "Because I wish to be a monk. Since I heard of thy fame, I let everything go and sought thee. Do not keep me from my desire." Rabban Sauma said to him: "My brother, this way is difficult and hardly can an elder man bear its difficulty; let go the thought that youths and children can tread it." And when he had given him much persuasion to return to his parents, but he did not change his mind, he accepted him as a disciple, and he clothed him with the wool [5] and set him to the service. After three years he received the tonsure, in other words the habit, from the holy man Mar Nestorios the Metropolitan [6] on the Sunday of the Holy Spirit the Paraclete [Whitsunday]. And he continued in many toils and fastings lasting till evening. And they were toiling in the mountain [12*] in the service of purity and holiness and taking comfort in God, to whom they had committed themselves.

[4] Hilgenfeld notes that this noun should be pointed as a plural, and that there must be a lacuna telling the story of some disputation.

[5] The garb of the monk. The Muslim Sufis took their name from a garment of wool, çûf.

[6] There had been a change in the Metropolitanship of China since the ordination recorded p. 7*.

[THE PILGRIMAGE OF RABBAN SAUMA AND RABBAN MARKOS
TOWARDS JERUSALEM]

One day they took counsel that "if we should leave this region
and go off to the West, it were dear to us to receive benediction
from the shrines of the Holy Martyrs and the Fathers Catholici,[1]
and if the Christ, the Lord of All, prolong our life and bring us on
the way by His grace, that we go to Jerusalem, so that we may
acquire perfect reconciliation for our sins and remission of our
faults." Although Rabban Sauma held Rabban Markos back and
was terrifying him with the difficulty of the way and the fatigue
of the journey and the danger of the roads and the obstacles one
might find [13*] in a foreign land, Rabban Markos was hot to go,
and revealed to him his mind that as it were treasures were in store
for him in the West. And he kept urging Rabban Sauma with his
arguments and impelling him to the departure. And when they
had agreed that neither would separate from the other, even if
he should have to bear for his sake any kind of hurt, they rose
up and distributed their fleece garments and vessels among the
poor, and entered into that [the neighboring] city so as to get
companions for the journey and furnish themselves with pro-
visions. The Christians there at once recognized them and learned
their purpose and gathered to them, so as to turn them from their
purpose, saying: "Perhaps you know not how great is the distance
of the country you are going to, or how misleading the perplexity
of the roads, beyond your reckoning, so that you cannot arrive
there. Remain here and strive in the life to which you have been
called. For it is said that 'the Kingdom of Heaven is within you'
[Luke 17:21]." They replied "We have already put on [14*] the
habit and denied the world, for we are dead. We expect of it
no trouble that will terrify us, no fear to disturb us. One thing
we ask of you, that for the love of Christ you pray for us, and
that you give up talk that produces hesitation, and that ye seek
that the will of God be fulfilled." They said: "Go in peace."

---

[1] 'Catholicus' was the earlier title of the head of the Oriental Church, signifying
its dependence upon the Patriarchate of Antioch; see Badger, 1, c. 11. Both titles,
Catholicus and Patriarch, are often used together.

And they kissed one another, and they separated with anguished weeping and affecting cries, saying: "Go in peace. Our Lord, whom you seek, be with you, and provide for you what seems best to Him and is helpful to you. Amen."

And they came to the city Koshang. And when the citizens and the parents of Rabban Markos had heard that these two monks were arrived, they went joyfully out to meet them and received them with joy and cheer, and with great honor did they bring them into the church. And they asked them: "How is it you have come?", for they thought they were going to remain with them, and that Rabban Markos had done this because of the proximity [15*] of his family. But when they affirmed that they were going to Jerusalem and were fixed on the West, and were on the way, they felt it greatly and were much grieved. Now the news came to the lords of the city, who were sons-in-law of the Khan King of Kings, namely, Kunbogha and Ifogha.[2] And upon the news they sent messengers and brought the two monks to the Camp.[3] And they received them with pleasure, and the light of love for them was kindled within them. When they learned that "they are leaving us," they began to say to them: "Why do you leave our region and go to the West? For we are very anxious to draw monks and fathers from the West to this region. How can you let yourselves go away?" Rabban Sauma answered: [16*] "We have let the world go, and so far as we are with men we do not find rest. And so it is right for us to flee away for the love of the Christ, who gave Himself to the death for our redemption. Whatever is in the world we have cast behind, although your love for us urges us not to go, and your kindnesses constrain us, and your alms are abundantly shed upon us, and it is even agreeable to us to dwell with you. We recall the Lord's word:

---

[2] The title would indicate Kublai, who according to Polo, ii, c. 9, had forty-seven sons, the names of twelve of whom, with the title of king, have been preserved, and with no count of daughters. But Pelliot, *T'oung Pao*, 15, 631 *et seq.*, can identify these princes; they are known chiefs of the Christian Ongut Turks, Kunbuqa and Aibuqa, whose family relationships are a matter of history; the latter is the father of 'Prince George,' who figures in Marco Polo as a descendant through his mother of Prester John.

[3] The old nomadic term for the court; see note at p. 3*; and so frequently below of the Ilkhan court.

'What does it profit a man if he gain the whole world and lose his own soul, and what will a man give in exchange for his soul?' [Matt. 16:26]. Although we desire the separation, yet wherever we are, in proportion to our weakness, we shall remember your kingdom with prayers night and day."

When they saw that argument with them was useless and that they would not yield to persuasion, they distributed to them gifts, equipment, gold and silver and garments. But they said: "We need nothing. For what can we do with possessions, [17*] and how can we burden ourselves with this great load?" Then the Kings answered: "Then you are not acquainted with the length of the road and the expense it demands. But we know, and we advise you not to go empty-handed. You are not able to reach your destination without funds. And so accept these gifts from us as loans, and if cause of poverty calls, spend them, and if you arrive in safety, distribute them to the monasteries and convents of the monks there and the fathers, so that we may have fellowship with our fathers of the West. For it is said: 'Your abundance for their want' [2 Cor. 8:14]." Then these monks, when they saw that they gave with a pure heart, took what the Kings gave. And they parted from one another sorrowfully, and weeping mixed with joy followed them.

And thence they came to the city Tanguth.[4] [18*] And the citizens heard that Rabban Sauma and Rabban Markos were come on their way to Jerusalem. They went forth with ardor to meet them, men and women, youths and striplings, boys and girls. For very ardent was the faith of the people of Tanguth

[4] According to Polo, i, c. 40, this is the name of an extensive province at the north-west end of China; it is to be identified with the present province of Kansu (Yule, p. 199). The city at which Polo arrived from the West he calls Sachiu, which Yule (ib.) identifies with modern S(h)achau, on the edge of the desert, where Polo notes he found some Christians. But the city of Tanguth as above is probably Kanchau (modern An-hsi-chau), which was on Pauthier's testimony the chief city of Kan-su. It is identified with Polo's Campichu, c. 44 (see Yule's discussion), in which city he found 'three very fine churches.' It was these Christians who welcomed our pilgrims. However, Bonin, Journ. as., series ix, vol. 15 (1900), 584 et seq., regards Tanguth as embracing all West China, including Shen-si, and the ancient capital Sin-gan-fu, the site of the Nestorian Stone. The pilgrims would then have been at the mother-church of China. The name Tanguth is admitted by the scholars to be indefinite in its extent.

and pure their intention. And they honored them with all kinds
of gifts, and they received their benedictions. And crowds followed them, weeping and saying: "Our Lord who chose you for
the honor of His service, He will be with you. Amen."

Thence they came to Loton[5] after two months' journey in the
vexation and trouble of that cold desert; for it was void of inhabitants because the water was bitter, and it was not sown at all,
and scarcely in an eight days' journey was there found sweet
water to load the wagons [?].[6] And at the time they arrived at
Loton there happened to be a quarrel between the Khan King of
Kings [19*] and King Oko.[7] And the latter fled from him and
came to the place and destroyed a thousand people there, and the
roads and paths were cut off, and corn failed and was not to be had,
and many died of hunger and perished. And after six months the
monks went forth thence, and they came to Kashgar.[8] And they
found the city emptied of its inhabitants, for it had been despoiled
by the enemy. But because their aim was fixed and they pleased
God with all their heart, He averted from them every disturber,
and suffering befell them not, and He saved them from captivity
and robbers. And they arrived at the court of King Kaidu [9]

[5] Bedjan, followed by Chabot, regards this name as error for Khotan, an important
city in the southwest of Eastern (Chinese) Turkestan, and a Metropolitan see. Polo
describes it, i, c. 36. There has been much recent exploration of this interesting
region; see especially the monumental work by A. Stein, *Ancient Khotan*, 2 vols.,
Oxford, 1907.

[6] Reading *redônê*, for *râdôyê* 'runners.' This desert is that of Lob, or Lop,
in Eastern Turkestan. Polo, i, c. 39, describes its terrors (the worst of them demons!)
and its lack of water—"in some 28 places altogether you will find water," and he
states that it took his party a month to make the transit. Yule in his note finds it
difficult to reconcile this with our maps. But our pilgrims, going much slower, took
double that time. Sven Hedin vividly describes his hazardous journey through the
same Great Desert, *My Life as an Explorer*, 1925, cc. 35 *et seq*.

[7] This person may be 'King Nogodar,' a bandit knight, who was operating in
these regions during Polo's travel eastwards; he himself was nearly caught by 'those
scoundrels'; see bk. i, c. 8, and the accompanying extensive note by Yule, pp. 96 *et seq*.
Cf. also Chabot. But Pelliot, *T'oung Pao*, 15, 632, corrects the reading to Alugu.

[8] An important city in the west of Eastern Turkestan; see Polo, i, c. 33, with
Yule's note, and Stein, *Khotan*, cc. 3, 4. It was a Metropolitan see of the Nestorians
and an important provincial capital; the awfulness of those wars appears in the present
account of its desolation.

[9] Kaidu was a grandson of Ogotay, the second Great Khan, who was able to main-
tain his independence of Kublai in Turkestan. In 1269 his forces invaded the Ilkhan

at Teleos.[10]   And they came to him and prayed for the preservation of his life and blessed his kingdom.   And they asked him for orders that none should injure them in his land.   But hardly, [20*] with the fatigue that accompanies fear, did they reach Khorasan,[11] abandoning on the way a lot of what they had with them.   And they came to the holy convent of Mar Sehyon [12] in the neighborhood of the city Tus.[13]   And they were blessed by the clergy and monks in that place, and so they thought that they were born afresh to the world.   And they acknowledged the grace of God on whom they trusted and in whom they hoped and rejoiced, for He is the aid and helper of all who seek Him.

And when they had delighted themselves in converse with those brethren, they started towards Adharbaijan,[14] that they might go thence to Baghdad to the Reverend Catholicus Denha.   But it happened that the Reverend Catholicus came to Marágha,[15] and

territories, and Polo has some romantic stories about him; see Howorth, *The Mongols*, I, 173–181; Yule, Index, *s. v.*

[10] This name has been identified by Chabot, after Klaproth, with the river and city Talas in Trans-Jaxartes. The following extract from Le Strange, *Eastern Caliphate*, 487, serves to identify the place with the capital of King Kaidu: " The ruins of Almaligh, which was the Mongol capital under Jaghatay [Ogotay] have been found near the site of Old Kuljah, on the river Ilih; and its position is indicated by Ali of Yazd, who also mentions the Irtish river and Tulâs [evidently our Telôs]." A fuller note on the place, with more exact location, is given by Yule-Cordier, *Cathay*, 3, 87, n. 1; its location is given in the map opposite p. 23 *ibid.* Bretschneider, *Mediæval Researches*, 2, 33–39, and vol. 1, note 172, gives a full treatment of Almaligh, especially from the Chinese sources,=Chinese A-li-ma-li. For Telos see *ib.*, vol. 1, notes 23, 585, on Talas or Taras, river and city, which the Chinese knew as Telosz, hence approving the spelling above. Our travellers' route, Khotan to Telos-Almaligh, was often taken by the Chinese travellers to the West in the 13th century, whose stories are given by Bretschneider, *e.g.*, vol. 1, 17, 69. Devéria records, *Journ. as.*, ser. ix, vol. 8, 421, 423, the establishment there of a Latin bishopric in 1338 and its destruction in 1342.

[11] The great eastern province of the old Abbaside domain; the travellers were now in the Ilkhan territory. See Le Strange, cc. 27–30.

[12] Chabot knows of no such saint. But Sehyon=Zion, and the combination with Mar is like our 'St. Saviour's.'

[13] One of the chief cities of Khorasan, and an episcopal see; see Le Strange, pp. 388 *et seq.*

[14] The province lying between the Caspian and the northeast of present Iraq, including Lake Urmia.

[15] Bedjan prefers the spelling Margha after one MS. This is the name of a bishopric in the Jezîrah province (Upper Mesopotamia), whence came the celebrated Thomas of Margha. But the place meant here is Mârâghâ, east of Lake Urmia,

they met him there. And their joy was great, and their exultation increased, and their mind was made peaceful, and they were relieved of their concern in seeing him. And they fell on the ground before him, prostrating and praying, [21*] and it was as if they saw our Lord Jesus Christ in the person of Mar Denha the Catholicus—his memory be for blessing! For they said to him: "His mercy is great to us and His grace is shed upon us, that we have seen the glorious and spiritual person of our Catholic Father." And when he asked them, "Whence are ye?", they replied: "From the regions of the East, from Khan-balek [sic], the city of the Khan King of Kings, have we come, to receive benedictions from you and the fathers and the monks and the saints of this region. And if the road allows, and God is merciful to us, we shall go to Jerusalem." And when the Catholicus saw their tears mingled with joy at meeting him, his compassion was stirred up for them, and he encouraged them, and said to them: "In truth, my sons, the Angel of Solicitude will guard you on this difficult journey, and he will be your guide until the fulfillment of your quest. Grieve not at your toils, for it is said in the Prophet, [22*] 'They who sow in tears shall reap in joy' [Ps. 126:5]. You shall attain your hope, and for the sufferings and afflictions you have endured reward and pay double and full shall you receive in this world, and in that to come happiness which passes not away and pleasures which never end." They did obeisance to him and made him their acknowledgments.

And when they had delighted themselves in converse with him for a few days, they made request of him, that "if we find mercy in the eyes of the Reverend Father, may he permit us to go to Baghdad, that we may receive a benediction from the holy shrines of Mar Mari the Apostle, the Teacher of the East,[16] and from the shrines of the fathers there; and thence to the convents in the lands

---

seventy miles south of Tabriz, which under the Mongols was the capital of Adharbaijan, and in the neighborhood of which the kings had their Camp, as the data below show. See Le Strange, pp. 164 et seq. The Catholicus had doubtless come on diplomatic business with the court. The neighboring Tabriz was the Ilkhan commercial metropolis and the nucleus of trade between East and West.

[16] The traditional colleague of Addai and Apostle of Iraq; see notices upon him in Assemani, c. 4, and more fully in Abbeloos in his publication of Acta S. Maris, Brussels, 1885. See further p. 23*.

of Beth-garmai [17] and Nisibis [18] to receive benediction and to ask help." When the Catholicus saw the loveliness of their intention and the sincerity of their mind and the fixedness of their purpose, he said to them: "Go, my sons, the Christ, Lord of All, grant you your request [23*] out of His rich and overflowing treasury, and fulfill His grace with you, and His favor follow you wheresoever you go." And he wrote letters patent for them to those places, that wherever they went they should be honored; and he sent with them a man to show them the way and to guide them on the roads.

And they arrived at Baghdad, and thence to the Great Church of Kôkê.[19] And they came to the monastery of Mar Mari the Apostle. And they received benedictions from the shrines of that country. And from there they turned and came to the country of Beth-garmai. From its shrine, full of the works and cures of Mar Hezkiel [20] they received the benediction. And thence they went to Arbel,[21] and thence to Mosul. And they moved on to Shighar [22] and to Nisibis and to Merda.[23] And they received

[17] Beth-garmai was the Metropolitan district on the Upper Zab, northeast of Mosul, one of the great centres of Nestorian monastic life; see Assemani, iii, pt. 2, 747 et seq., 874, and for its schools, p. 931; Hoffmann, Auszüge, 253 et seq.

[18] Modern Nisibin, once the seat of the most distinguished of Nestorian academies, the successor of the ruined School of Edessa; see Assemani, p. 927; J. B. Chabot, 'L'École de Nisibis,' Journ. as., ser. ix, vol 8, 43–93; G. F. Moore, in the Toy Volume, Studies in the History of Religions, 255 et seq.; Baumstark, Gesch. d. syr. Lit., 113 et seq.

[19] This was the ancient See church (sometimes called 'the Great Church') of the Patriarchate at Seleucia-Ctesiphon, the Arabic Al-Madain ('Double-City'), which still retained its primitive primacy, despite the removal of the actual location of the See to Baghdad (even as the Archbishops of Canterbury reside officially in London); see Assemani, pp. 622 et seq., 628, etc. (also i, 10); Sachau, Ausbreitung d. Christentums, 26 et seq. It is often named in the Liturgies, e.g., Assemani, p. 674, Badger, 2, 340, as great functions, like Patriarchal consecrations, were always held there. Presumably all traces of it have now disappeared. Koke appears to have been the original name of the site of the old capital; see Abbeloos, Acta S. Maris, 48, note. Mari was buried near Koke at Dur-qoni; see Assemani, p. 128, Abbeloos, p. 72, note. For the obscure history of the rise of the Patriarchate see Assemani, i, 9 et seq., and the critical discussions in J. Labourt, Le christianisme dans l'empire perse, 1904, cc. 1, 2, and F. Haase, Altchristliche Gesch. nach oriental. Quellen. 1925, 91–110.

[20] A monastery at Dakok named after its founder; see Budge, Thomas of Margha, i, p. lxxvii.

[21] The Assyrian and Classical Arbela.

[22] Arabic Sinjar, to the west of Mosul; see Le Strange, p. 98.

[23] Modern Mardin; ib., p. 96.

benediction from the shrine of the bones of Mar Augen, the Second Christ.[24] And from there to the Island of Beth-zabdai.[25] And from all the shrines and monasteries (that is, convents)[26] and the monks and fathers in those places they received benedictions. And they paid the vows for which they were bounden, [24*] and assigned tables [for the poor] and did alms wherever they came. And they turned back and came to the holy convent of Mar Michael of Tar'el.[27] And they bought a cell, and the two of them were received by the monks there. And the purpose which was operating in them stayed from its course, although they had not attained the object of their expectation.

When Mar Denha the Catholicus heard of the manner of their life, he sent and required them to come to him. And they went at once and gave the greeting of the monastery. And he said to them: "We have heard that you have been received in a monastery, but it does not please us that you should live a conventual life. In this way you will obtain only surcease for yourselves. But living with us, you will gain profit and satisfaction for the community. And so do you stay with us and assist in the royal court [lit. 'gate'] in whatsoever chances to your hands." They said to him: "Whatever [25*] our Father bids us we will do." He said to them: "Go to King Abaga.[28] You will receive commissions for us." They said to him: "So be it. But let our Reverend Father send a man with us who will take the commissions and give them to him." And he prevailed on them in this matter, and furnished them with blessings [recommendations?]. And when they came to the Blessed Camp,[29] an emir presented them to

---

[24] Augen-Eugenios, the founder of monastic life among the Nestorians; he established a convent at Mount Izla near Nisibis in Tur Abdin. See Assemani, pp. 862 et seq.; Hoffmann, pp. 168, 171. His Acts have been published by Bedjan in Acta martyrum et sanctorum, iii. His epithet, remarkable indeed, is otherwise known; see Payne Smith, Thes. syr. 2241.

[25] Beth-zabdai was a district on the right bank of the upper Tigris with Jazîrat ibn Omar as capital. The Syriac word here, gazartha = Arabic jazîrat, means 'island,' and is used of districts almost surrounded by water. See Assemani, pp. 730, 732; Le Strange, p. 93.

[26] Syriac diction often interpolates a variant word otiose.

[27] Bedjan locates this monastery near Mosul.

[28] Died 1281; see Int., § ii.

[29] As appears below, the royal residence was to the east of Lake Urmia. Such

the King, and he asked them about the manner of their coming and what was their country. And they gave him an answer which revealed their purpose.[30] Then he ordered his officials to fulfill their quest, and to give them orders as they required, and the commission which the Reverend Catholicus required of them they forwarded with his messenger.

And they started out with companions to Jerusalem. And when they reached the city Animto [31] [26*] and saw the convents and monasteries there, they marvelled at the size of their construction and their beauty. And thence they went to Bethgorgaye,[32] that they might go by a clear road. But when they arrived there, they learned from the citizens that the road was cut off by reason of the murders and depredations which occurred in it.

[APPOINTMENT OF RABBAN MARKOS YABALLAHA AS METROPOLITAN AND OF RABBAN SAUMA AS VISITATOR-GENERAL]

And they turned back and came to the Reverend Catholicus. And he was glad for them, and said to them: "It is not the time to go to Jerusalem, for the roads are disturbed and the routes cut off. But you have received benedictions from all the houses of God and the monasteries [27*] in them [?]. And to my mind when one visits these with a pure heart, the service to them is not less than reaching Jerusalem. And I give you fitting counsel, worthy of your heed. I have decided to make Markos Metropolitan and to devolve the Apostolic gifts upon him; and thou, Rabban Sauma, I will appoint thee Visitator-General. And I will send you to your several places." Those monks answered and said: "The word of

titles as 'blessed' are applied to Christian cities, and it is significant that the term is here applied to the Camp.

[30] This official may well be the Emir Asmoth, who later, according to Bar Hebræus, called the royal attention to Markos as a likely appointee for the Patriarchate; see Int., § iv.

[31] Bedjan, by a rearrangement of the letters and construction, ingeniously suggests the city Ani, the old capital of Christian Armenia, and this agrees with the subsequent route. The ruins of its cathedral, citadel, etc., are among the most notable of Armenian remains.

[32] Syriac for Georgia. From the coast of this Christian state, probably *via* Trebizond (as on the subsequent mission to the West and so Polo on his return), they intended to ship by the Black and Mediterranean Seas to the Holy Land, the land routes being closed. For the importance of that city in Oriental trade see W. Heyd, *Gesch. d. Levantehandels im Mittelalter*, 2, 95–108.

our Reverend Father is by the command of the Christ, and whoever does not execute it contributes to the transgression of the command. But herewith we reveal our mind and declare our inward heart. We did not come from there to go back there [*i.e.*, to China]. Nor are we minded along with the difficulty we have endured again a second time to endure it. For it were foolish to be weighed down with a stone twice. [28*] And further we say that we are not worthy of this gift, and for small men such an assignment is difficult. And what we ask is this, that we remain in the convent and serve the Christ until we die." And the Catholicus said to them: "This gift is fit for you and the assignment worthy of your modesty." And when they saw that their apology was not seemly, they said: "The will of our Father be done." And he said: "Till now Rabban Markos has not been given a name. I will therefore give him a name in this wise, proposing this, that we write the [eligible] names and place them on the altar, and the one which comes forth by the hand of the one to be known by it, with that shall we name him." And he did so. And there came forth the name Yaballaha.[1] And he said that "this is from the Lord, blessed be He!" And they qualified. And Rabban Markos received the degree of Metropolitan from Mar Denha the Catholicus in the 35th year of his age [29*] for the diocese of Kathi and of Ong.[2]

And after a few days there came the news that the road they had come by [from China] was completely cut off and none was following it, because the mind of the two Kings of the two regions on either side of the Gihon[3] was changed [towards one another].

[1] *I.c.*, 'God has given.' He was the third Patriarch of this name.

[2] Kathi (rather Kathay, with change of the Syriac pointing) is Polo's Cathay, as the name still exists for China in Russian. The second name has been variously identified. Devéria, p. 408, note 1, interprets as Uighur 'the right,' *i.e.*, the Orient. But best is the identification, after Pelliot, with Ong, plural Ongut, the White Tartars of the Chinese, situated to the northwest of Shen-si, connecting China with Mongolia; see Howorth, *Mongols*, 1, 26, Pelliot, *T'oung Pao*, 15, 629 *et seq.* This appointment of Yaballaha to the Metropolitanship of China followed a scandal in that jurisdiction. A certain Simeon Bar-kalig had been ordained bishop of China in 1279, then had shown himself refractory, was imprisoned by the ecclesiastical authorities, and was later found dead in prison; see Bar Hebræus, *Chron. eccles.*, ii, 451, cited by Assemani, p. 112. The faction later made against the Patriarch Yaballaha may have been a sequel of these old troubles. The next paragraph tells why the two ecclesiastics did not return to China.

[3] *I.e.*, the Oxus, to which the Saracens gave the name of the Gihon, one of the

And so these illuminated men turned off to the convent of Mar Michael at Tar'el, and dwelt in their own cell for two years more or less.

One night when Mar Yaballaha was asleep, he saw a dream, as though he went into a great church, and in the church pictures of the Saints, [30*] and among them the Cross; and he stretched forth his hand to be blessed by it. And as much as he stretched forth his hand it was lengthening out, and the Cross was mounting up until it reached the top of the great nave, and there he caught and kissed it. And when he went out from the church, he saw high trees, laden with various fruits. And he began to take of the fruits and to feed himself from them, and he gave and administered them to the great throng that had assembled. And when he awoke he declared to Rabban Sauma that "I have seen a dream, and it terrified me." Rabban Sauma said to him: "Tell it to me." And when he had told it, Rabban Sauma interpreted it: "In that thy arm was lengthened out when thou didst stretch it forth to receive a benediction from the Cross and the pictures of the Saints, thou shalt attain to the great stature of the Fathers. And in that thou atest of the fruit of the trees and didst feed it to the people, by the heavenly gift that has fallen upon thee and in which thou delightest shalt thou delight many peoples." And again on another night Mar Yaballaha saw another vision. [31*] It was as though he sat on a lofty throne, and there was assembled about him a great throng, and he was teaching. And when he spoke, his tongue lengthened out until it went a long way forth of his mouth, and it divided into three forks, on each fork appearing something like fire. And the people there were wondering and praising God. And when he awoke, he again told it to Rabban Sauma. And he said to him: "This is not a dream, but a revelation, and like a revelation. For it is not at all to be distinguished from the Spirit which in the likeness of fiery tongues descended upon the Apostles. Also upon thee has the Spirit of Holiness descended. And the Patriarchal See will be given into thy hand to accomplish its ministry and to serve its function."[4]

four rivers of Paradise, Gen. 2; similarly the Jews had applied it to the Nile. See Le Strange, p. 434. The conflict is doubtless that between the Ilkhans and the rebellious Kaidu; see p. 19*.

[4] Cf. the story of a similar prophecy of Yaballaha's elevation in the Arabic Biography, given at the end of Int., § iv.

[ELECTION OF MAR YABALLAHA AS PATRIARCH]

[32*] And when these things took place, Mar Denha the Catholicus was still alive; but he was stricken with a disease in Baghdad. Moreover many of the monks and the fathers were seeing dreams like those. And a few days after the purpose moved in Yaballaha to go to Baghdad to the Catholicus, to receive the benediction, the *biron* [1] and the staff, that they might accompany him to his place. And when he arrived at Holy Baghdad, there met him one of his acquaintance, who said to him: "The Catholicus is deceased. And if perchance thou wert urgent for thy belongings, thou wouldest have come to him before his departure." Then in great sorrow and with anxious heart he started off hastily, and at last he reached the door of the church. And when he entered he saw great crowds weeping, [33*] and others praying. He went up to the bier, and he took off his mitre and tore his clothes and wept with bitter sobs. And at last he fell on the ground as dead. And after an hour they raised him up and put his mitre on him and comforted him. And when the service was finished, he [the Patriarch] was buried—his memory be for a blessing! And the fathers returned to their cells.

When the next day came, the fathers assembled to choose a person who should sit on the Throne. And there were of these: first Maran-ammeh, Metropolitan of Elam;[2] another, he of Tanguth;[3] another, he of Tirahan;[4] another, he of the Mountain;[5] and along with them the chiefs and scribes and lawyers and physicians of Baghdad.[6] And one said that it should be this, and another that,

[1] The colored habit of the Patriarch and Metropolitans; see Assemani, p. 666.

[2] He appears in Assemani's list, as Metropolitan of Gandisapor, *v. inf.*, p. 38*, note 19. As p. 37* indicates, this bishop had the precedence in consecration of the Patriarch.

[3] See note to p. 17*.

[4] Tirhan is the name of a district in the neighborhood of Samarra in Iraq (see Hoffmann, pp. 188-191, Le Strange, p. 54), which according to Assemani, p. 785, was an episcopal see. Chabot prefers identification with Teheran near Ray in Persia; but Assemani does not record that city among the episcopal sees, Ray being the name of that diocese. The Arabic biography also reads Tirhan. The bishop of Tirhan appears subsequently as a consecrator of Yaballaha, p. 38*, note 19.

[5] With Chabot=Tur ('Mount') Abdin, north of Nisibis, the mountainous district famous as the great monastic centre; see note at p. 23*, and *cf.* Hoffmann, p. 167.

[6] For the election of the Patriarch see Assemani, pp. 643 *et seq.* The Christian

until at last they all agreed that Mar Yaballaha should be the
head and leader for the See of Seleucia-Ctesiphon.[7] [34*] The
reason of his election was this. The Rulers of the whole empire
were Mongols, and there was none who was acquainted at all with
their customs and policies and language but he.[8] And when
they told him this, he begged off from it, and alleged that "I am
lacking in education and Church doctrine, and the member of my
tongue is afflicted; and how can I become this? For I am not
even acquainted with your Syriac language, which is a matter
of universal necessity." And when they pressed their solicitation
upon him, he agreed to their decision and accepted. He was
given an unanimous vote by all the clergy and priests and magnates
and scribes and also the physicians in Baghdad. And he arose
and came to the holy convent of Mar Michael at Tarʿel with
Rabban Sauma. The monks had already heard of the decease
of the holy father Mar Denha; when Mar Yaballaha arrived, they
received him with joy and encouraged him. And they were
unanimous that he should be Catholicus. It was a divine motion
and an operation [35*] from Him; everything by necessity serves
His accomplishment. And when he spoke with Rabban Sauma, the
latter said to him: "This is the divine will, thou canst not beg off
from it. Therefore let us go to King Abaga, and if he agrees, we
shall receive ordination."

And they arose and went off to Adharbaijan, along with the
clergy and fathers and monks who accompanied them, because the
kings were summering there. And they came to the King at
Black Mountain [*Tura Ukkáma*], which is known in the Persian
as Seyacoh [= Siyáh Kuh].[9] And the emirs introduced them,
and they presented their petition: "The King live forever! The
Catholicus is deceased, and all the Christians have unanimously
agreed that this Metropolitan should take his place, one who came
from the East to go to Jerusalem. What does the King command?"

___

physicians of Baghdad were famous in the Oriental world and took high place in the
Church.

   [7] See note to p. 23*.

   [8] For the actual dictation of this election see Int., § iv.

   [9] As noted above Adharbaijan is the country southwest of the Caspian. The
Black Mountain is west of Ardabel, one of the chief cities; see Le Strange, p. 168.
The Mongol centre was at Marágha, see p. 20*, note 15.

And he answered: "Worthy of admiration is this purity [36*] of motive and conscience, and God is with those who seek Him and do His will. This man and his companion have come from the East to go to Jerusalem. This [the election] has happened to them by the will of God. We too serve the will of God and the prayers of the Christians. He shall stand as their head and sit upon the throne." And he took the hand of Mar Yaballaha and said to him: "Hail to thy administration, and God be with thee and help thee!" And he covered his head with the pallium,[10] for his pallium was thrown over his shoulders; and he gave him his own *sedile*,[11] which is a settee, and also a *shather*,[12] called in Mongolian *sukor*, which is put over the heads only of kings and queens and their children, to protect them from the force of sun and rain. And many things which they reserve for their own honor he gave him, and also a tablet,[13] which is a symbol of those kings; as also the customary letters, to wit, that he should have full jurisdiction, [37*] along with the great seal which had belonged to the Catholici before him, and in addition an appropriation for the great expenses required for the ordination he confirmed to him.[14]

Then they arose and went to Baghdad, and they came to the Church of Kôkê,[15] and Mar Yaballaha received the *cheirotonia*, that is, the ordination, so as to take the helm of government of the Oriental Church. And he sat on the throne of Seleucia and Ctesiphon; about him the holy father Maran-ammeh, Metropolitan of Elam, the Ordainer and Warden of the Apostolic See, and the

[10] Syr. *ma'phra*; the Jacobite Patriarch is hence called the Maphran; see Assemani, iii, pt. 2, 666.

[11] Syr. and Arab. *çandali*; see Löw, *Zeits. d. Deutsch. Morgenl. Gesells.*, 47, 517. For the silver chair of high officials see Polo, ii, 7, and Yule's note, p. 317.

[12] 'Shather,' evidently from a Sem. rt. = 'protect'; I do not find it in the dictionaries. This is the honorific umbrella of the Mongols, described by Polo, *ib.*, and see Yule's accompanying note. The same combination of the two terms appears p. 97*.

[13] Syriac *paiza*, a Persianized form of a probably Chinese word, *pai-tseu*. Polo, *l.c.*, gives a long account of these honorific tablets, generally of precious metal and appropriately inscribed, which constituted the diploma of rank; see Yule's long note, pp. 314 *et seq.*

[14] The necessary recognition of the Patriarch by royal letters patent was of old standing, dating back to the 10th century under the Caliphs; see Assemani, p. 663, with examples of such diplomas.

[15] See at p. 23*.

assembled fathers, of whom there were these: Mar Isho-zeká, Metropolitan of Suba [16] and Armenia; and Mar Moshe [Moses], Metropolitan of Arbel; and Mar Gabrel, Metropolitan of Mosul and Nineveh; and Mar Elia, Metropolitan of Dakok [17] and Beth-garmai; and Mar Abraham, Metropolitan of Turpelos [18] and Jerusalem; and Mar Jacob, Metropolitan of Samarkand; and Yohanan, [38*] Metropolitan of Adharbaijan, along with the other bishops to the number of twenty-four. The ordination took place in Second Tishri [November] on the first Sunday of Kuddash-edta, year 1593 of the Greek Era [= 1281 A. D.] in the 37th year of his age.[19]

It happened in the winter of that year that King Abaga came down to Baghdad, and Mar Yaballaha went to him on the Sabbath before the Dominical Fast [i.e., Lent] and set forth to him the activity of the Christians. And he found favor in his eyes, and he [the King] presented him with great gifts, and gave him an order to take every year for the churches and monasteries and monks and priests and deacons 30,000 dinars, which is 180,000 white zûz.[20] And he sent the Catholicus to recover this quantity of donation from the countries. [39*] But when that King departed from this temporal life, the donation was withdrawn.[21]

[16] I.e., Nisibis, with play on the Biblical Sobah; see Assemani, p. 767, Hoffmann, p. 292. The successor of this prelate in the same province in 1290 was the distinguished writer Abd-Isho.

[17] A town in Beth-garmai.

[18] Tripoli of Syria, still in Christian hands, the residence of the Metropolitan of Jerusalem; for this province see Sachau, Ausbreitung, 79, cf. p. 21.

[19] Kuddash-edta = 'Hallowing of the Church,' the name given to a series of Sundays corresponding to our Advent, beginning with the first Sunday in Second Tishri, approximately our November. For the Nestorian Calendar see Assemani, iii, pt. 2, 380 et seq., Neale, History of the Holy Eastern Church, 1850, pp. 729 et seq. The predecessor died Feb. 24, see Assemani, ii, 456. The long interim was occupied with the necessary negotiations and journeys. Assemani gives, ib., a fuller list of consecrating bishops, taken from Amr's Chronicle. He includes Maranammeh, see p. 33*, but described as Metropolitan of Gandisapor, in ancient Elam (Assemani, p. 745); Moshe of Arbel, Elia of Dakok and Abraham of Jerusalem as here. The bishops of Samarkand and Adharbaijan do not appear in his list, which gives twenty-one names.

[20] This tax was of course levied upon the Church by the royal authority. The dinar was worth a German mark; see Yule, 2, 285.

[21] Abaga appears to have been most friendly to the Christians; Bar Hebræus reports that within a year of his death he celebrated the Easter feast in the church at Baghdad; Chron. syr., 547 = Bruns, p. 593. And this must be the occasion reported above. See further for his character, Howorth, 3, 276.

[THE DIFFICULTIES IN THE REIGN OF AHMAD]

And not to prolong the story of what took place in the mean time, there arose in this King's stead his brother who was called Ahmad, son of King Hulagu [text, Hulabu]. Now he was lacking in education and knowledge, and he persecuted the Christians much by reason of his association with the Hagarenes.[1] And because two envious clergy found opportunity to accomplish their purpose, they entered the presence of King Ahmad through the intervention of certain Arabs [i.e., Muslims], one of the latter being named [40*] Shams ad-Din, officer of the budget [the Arabic word daiwan]—he was chief secretary of public accounts—the other an elder man, Abd ar-Rahman.[2] And they slandered Yaballaha the Catholicus and Rabban Sauma and accused them, that their heart was with Arghon son of King Abaga, and that "they have written and complained against thee, O King, to the Khan King of Kings [i.e., Kublai Khan]." And there was associated in the complaint Shammoth, who was then governor of the city of Mosul and its district—he was a monk and an ascetic ['Nazirite'].[3] And these two men named took Ahmad as an instrument to accomplish their desire through the agency of the aforesaid clergy, who were Isho-sabran, Metropolitan of Tanguth [4] and Shem'on Bishop of Arni.[5] These two men had the plan that the one should be Catholicus, the other Metropolitan and Visitator-General. And when by the counsel of the Devil [41*] this purpose occurred to them, they undertook this method, as we have recorded. The King

---

[1] I.e., Muslims, as descendants of Abraham and Hagar. This prince, a brother of Abaga, had a Tartar name, Tagodor, and showed himself at first most benevolent to the Christians; see Bar Hebræus, Chron. syr., 553 = Bruns, p. 593, and Assemani, p. 114. His adoption of the Muslim name Ahmad indicates his change of heart towards Islam.

[2] Bar Hebræus details Shams ad-Din's indictment against the Christians, Chron. eccl., pp. 562, 601 (cited by Chabot). The Christian author speaks of his ability in the highest terms, Chron. syr., 549 = Bruns, p. 597. The same history recounts the story of his death, effected by Abaga's son Arghon, on the ground that he had assassinated his father; p. 554 = Bruns, p. 603.

[3] See Payne Smith, s. v.

[4] Evidently a case of jealousy of this bishop of a Chinese jurisdiction against the Chinese monk who had been elevated as Catholicus.

[5] Modern Arna, in the neighborhood of Maragha; see Hoffmann, p. 204.

then, being lacking in education, for he had abandoned God, did
not consider that these men could have no satisfaction in such an
operation—what could they allege in their complaint? But he
believed the words of the deceivers, and by his orders Mar Yaballaha the Catholicus with Rabban Sauma and the emir Shammoth
was brought to the Great House.[6] In place of the orders he had
given for them he took away the house of the Reverend Catholicus
and the tablet. And when they entered the court they did not
know what would be required of them. And they remained aghast,
for "what then have we done?". For the messenger of the court,
who brought them in, said: "Your own clergy and clerks and
fellows of the Sacrament have accused you before the King." ·
Then the Chief Emir, that is the Judge, asked the Catholicus:
"What evil hast thou seen on part of the King that thou shouldst
be disloyal to him and shouldst send word to lay accusation with
the Khan King of Kings, to the effect that he [the King] had left
the way of [42*] his fathers and had become a Hagarene?" He
answered and said: "I am not privy to anything." They said:
"Thy clerks have said this against thee." And they brought
them in. And as each one was brought in by himself, each made
reply as he knew. The Reverend Catholicus said: "O Emir, what
do you? Turn back that messenger with whom the documents
came, and examine them. If this accusation against me be true,
let me die without clemency and in my own blood [i.e., for my own
guilt]. And if not, it is for you to judge and to take vengeance."
And the emirs accepted this plea and presented it to the King.
He sent after the messenger and took away from him all the documents near Khorasan.[7] And when the documents were opened
and read, and there was not found in them anything adequate
for an accusation at all, and the judges did not find any accusers,
on account of this we knew that they had taken them [the letters]
as a pretext. But the Catholicus remained in ward forty days
more [43*] or less, in great torment and bitter suffering and affliction every day, until at last God looked after him in His mercy
and he was rescued from death. For King Ahmad was furious at

[6] I.e., the royal offices; cf. the Turkish 'Sublime Porte.'

[7] Why the messenger had gone so far to the east is not evident, unless he wished
to make evasion with the documents.

him, and like one thirsty for a cool drink did he desire to shed his blood, except for the Angel of Solicitude, who conducted this holy See, and served himself of his mother [8] and the emirs and overruled him from the purpose he had.   And further by the word of those we have named the Catholicus found mercy in the King's eyes, and the latter gave to him [again] the commission and the tablet, and he gladdened his heart and restored him.

He then departed from him and went to the city Urmia.[9] And in the Church of Our Lady Mary he saw a dream, and he knew that he was not to see the King again.   And after some time he arrived at the city Maragha,[10] he with the clergy his accusers. And King Ahmad went with his forces to Khorasan, so as to seize King Arghon, son of King Abaga.   And he and the two persons already named [i.e., Shams ad-Din and Abd ar-Rahman] and the chiefs of the Arabs took counsel [44*] that when they had taken him, he should kill the rest of the princes and he should be caliph in Baghdad; also he should dispatch the Catholicus.   But his purpose turned out in vain and his intention bootless.[11]   The Lord puts away the plans of men and establishes His own purpose, removing kings and doing away with kings, but His Kingdom stands forever.   And his [Ahmad's] forces were dispersed, and most of them helped King Arghon; and he was taken and killed [A.D. 1284].

[8] This may indicate that Ahmad had a Christian mother, unless it be a loose term for the Queen Dowager, i.e., Maria Palæologa, wife of Abaga; see Int. § ii.

[9] The well-known city to the west of Lake Urmia, at that time a large and important place.

[10] See p. 20*, note 15.   Where the previous trial was held is not told; it may have been at the Camp.   In that case the Catholicus may have been domiciled at Urmia so as to be kept under surveillance.   The present journey must have been due to a summons in line with the machinations which are immediately described.

[11] A long account of this civil war is given in bk. iv, cc. 6 et seq., of Marco Polo (Yule, 2, 398 et seq.);.cf. Bar Hebræus, Chron. syr., 551 et seq.=Bruns, pp. 601 et seq. According to this story Ahmad had seized the succession to his brother Abaga in the absence of the latter's son Arghon who was warring in Khorasan against a rebel to his father.   The nephew proceeded with an army against the usurper; he was defeated and taken prisoner.   But released by his powerful friends he again raised an army against Ahmad, and the latter fleeing was caught and put to death.   Ahmad was evidently supported by the Muslim party, and the reference to the caliphate at Baghdad which he was to assume indicates the plan of reviving that ancient institution under a Muslim Mongol prince.

Now on a night before the report of this news of what happened to King Ahmad, Mar Yaballaha the Catholicus saw a dream: that the like of a beautiful youth came to him carrying a platter in his hands, covered with veils, and he said to him, "Arise and eat what is placed therein." And when he took off the veils he found therein a boiled head. And when he had eaten and finished it and left the jaw-bones, the youth said to him: "Knowest thou [45*] what thou hast eaten?" He said, "No." The youth said to him: "This was the head of King Ahmad."[12] And at once the Catholicus awoke in fear. And after a few days came the news of the destruction of the aforesaid, and that King Arghon had become king. And his joy was increased, not for the death of that one but for the accession of this.

In those days he went with the clergy and monks to give his benediction to King Arghon, and also to satisfy the duties incumbent upon Christians to kings, whoever they are, according to the apostolic commands that 'every soul shall be subject to the power' of the country, 'for there is no power unless it be of God' [Rom. 13, 1]. And when he saw King Arghon and blessed him, he prayed for the permanence of his sovereignty. He [the King] increased his honor and exalted his station, when he heard of what happened to him at the hand of the King before him, and also the story of those clergy, whom we have named, who served with him, and he ordered their destruction. But Mar Yaballaha [46*] the Catholicus said: "O King, live forever! We Christians have laws, and when anyone does not fulfill them it is called a transgression. For our law does not inflict the death of a man but condemnation. And there are many categories of this [condemnation], and it [the process] is made use of by those who discipline sinners. And as for these clergy death is not their penalty by our law, but full dismissal from the rank with whose function they have been entrusted." And so it seemed good to the King, and he dismissed the Catholicus with great honor. And in joy he returned to his convent with much gladness.

And when the holy fathers were assembled with the Catholicus to welcome and encourage him, there was inquisition into the

[12] Chabot connects this theme with an Oriental expression in which 'eating the head' of an enemy means accomplishing his ruin.

history of those aforesaid men, and they decided after much inquisition, and after these had confessed their sinfulness, upon the sentence of deposition against them both, and they were dismissed from all the ecclesiastical orders.

[47*] [ABOUT THE JOURNEY OF RABBAN SAUMA TO THE LAND OF THE ROMANS IN THE NAME OF KING ARGHON AND THE CATHOLICUS MAR YABALLAHA]

Now Mar Yaballaha was advanced in his [the King's] presence, and day by day his honor increased before the King and the Queen.[1] For he pulled down the Church of Mar Shallita in Maragha and restored it at great expense, and replacing the [roof] timbers he made it into two naves.[2] At the side he made the cell of its vicar. And his affection was very warm for the family of King Arghon, because he loved the Christians with all his heart. And he was minded to go and subjugate the lands of Palestine and Syria: "that if the Western Kings, who are Christians, do not help me, my desire cannot be fulfilled."[3] So he desired of the Catholicus that he should give him a wise man, [48*] one useful and fit for the embassy, to send him to those Kings. And when the Catholicus saw that there was none acquainted with the languages except Rabban Sauma, since he was competent for this, he commissioned him to go.

Then Rabban Sauma said: "I am desirous of this and eager for it." And King Arghon at once wrote recommendations for him to the Kings, to the Kings of the Greeks and the Franks, that is, the Romans, and *yarliks*[4] and letters, with gifts for each King separately. And he gave Rabban Sauma 2000 pounds of gold,[5]

---

[1] Arghon had two Christian wives; or the term may refer to the Dowager Maria Palæologa; see Int. § ii, and *cf.* p. 42*, note 8.

[2] Such appears to be the meaning; he replaced the flat wooden roof with two vaulted naves.

[3] The King would be baptized only in Jerusalem; see Int. § ii. The Pope's letter to him (Raynald, *an.* 1288, no. 36) argues at length with him upon the absolute and immediate necessity of baptism. The Biographer ignores the earlier mission sent to the West by Arghon in the second year of his reign.

[4] 'Yarlik,' a Mongol word, meaning a letter patent, generally the document accompanying the gift of the *paiza*; see Yule, 1, 314.

[5] I so translate for convenience the Syriac word *mathqela*, primarily 'weight.' For

along with thirty goodly steeds and a tablet. And when he came to the monastery to receive a letter from Mar Yaballaha the Catholicus and to bid him adieu, the Catholicus gave him his permission to go. [49*] And when the time of departure came, he [the Catholicus] was unhappy, for he said: "What will become of this? For thou hast been the manager of the monastery, and thou knowest well that with thy departure my undertakings will fall into confusion." And after he had spoken thus they separated from one another with weeping. And documents and presents that were befitting he sent with him to the Reverend Pope, gifts commensurate to his ability.

[RABBAN SAUMA IN BYZANTIUM]

And Rabban Sauma started off, and there went with him certain eminent priests and deacons of the monastery. He arrived at the land of the Romans [1] on the shores of the sea . . .[2] And he saw the church. And he embarked in a ship. And his companions with him in the ship were more than 300 souls.[3] And every day he used to exhort them with a discourse on the Faith. And many of the people in the ship were Romans [i.e., Greeks], and by reason of the flavor of his discourse they honored him not a little.

And after some days he reached the great city of Constantinople. [50*] And before he entered, he sent two pages to the royal court to announce that King Arghon's ambassador was come. And the King commanded that certain should go out to meet them and bring them in with joy and honor. And when Rabban Sauma entered, he appointed a house, that is a mansion, for his

calculations of the value of the mediæval pound see Yule 2, 471, and 1, 48. The corresponding Arabic *mithqâl* is generally used of the dinar.

[1] 'Rome' was the current Oriental name of the Byzantine Empire, which controlled the Black Sea ports.

[2] Syriac *demekka*, i.e., 'on this side,' which is nonsense. Chabot proposes, with a different pointing, *de-meka*, i.e., the Greek word *mega*, 'great,' as the Black Sea was then known; or possibly *damka*, 'quiet,' euphemistically, like 'Euxine.' The port in question is doubtless Trebizond, p. 26*, note 32.

[3] Yule, pp. lx-lxix, discusses the shipping of the age. He notes that a war-galley might have a complement of more than 250 men.

stay. And after he was rested, he came to King Basilios.[4] And after he greeted him, the King asked him: "How art thou after the fatigue of the sea and the weariness of the journey?" He answered: "With the sight of the Christian King weariness is banished and fatigue dismissed. For I was eager to see your kingdom, which Our Lord preserve!"

And after they were regaled with food and drink, he desired of the King that he might see the churches and the shrines of the fathers and the relics of the saints there. The King put him in the hands of his royal officers, and they showed him everything [51*] that was there. First, he went into the great Church of Sophia, which has 360 gates,[5] which are all finished in marble. And the dome over the altar it is impossible to describe to one who has not seen it, or to tell the extent of its height and width. There is in the church a picture of the Lady Mary, which Luke the Evangelist painted.[6] And he saw too the hand of John Baptist, and the relics of Lazarus and Mary Magdalen,[7] and the stone that was set upon Our Lord's tomb, when Joseph the Counsellor took Him down from the Cross; and Mary wept on that stone and to the present her tears are moist, and as often as its moisture is wiped off, it becomes moist again.[8] Moreover he saw the jar of stone in which Our Lord changed the water to wine [52*] at Cana of Galilee; and the sarcophagus of one of the holy women, which is brought forth every year, and every sick person who is placed under it is healed; [and] the sarcophagus of John Chrysostom. And he saw the stone on which Simon Peter sat when the cock crew; and the tomb of the Victorious King Constantine, which is

---

[4] I.e., Greek basileus, 'king.' The emperor was Andronikos II. For the adverse policy of the Byzantine court at this time towards any comity with the West see The Cambridge Medieval History, 4, c. 19.

[5] The figure is absurd; probably pillars are meant. Is there confusion between Greek stoa and the Oriental word eston, 'pillar'?

[6] We know of a picture of the Virgin Mary at Constantinople, which was, however, stolen by the Venetians at the Latin capture of the city in 1204, for which act of sacrilege Pope Leo issued a bull against them in 1207. For the sacred treasures which had been amassed in Constantinople the chief authority is Riant, Exuviæ sacræ constantinopolitanæ, Geneva, 1887–1888.

[7] In the Church of SS. Lazarus and Mary.

[8] This stone was shown in the Fourth Crusade (Chabot).

reddish;[9] and the tomb of Justinian, which is of a green color; and the stations of the 318 Fathers [of the Council of Nicæa], which are all set in one large church, and their bodies are not corrupted because they confirmed the Faith; and also many shrines of the holy fathers. And he saw many amulets, and ikons figured in bronze and stone.

Then Rabban Sauma went in to King Basilios and said: "The King live forever! I acknowledge the grace of Our Lord in that I have been deemed worthy of the sight of these holy shrines. And now, if the King permits, I will proceed to fulfill the orders of [53*] King Arghon, his orders that I go to the lands of the Franks." Then the King treated him kindly and presented him with gifts of gold and silver.

[Rabban Sauma in Italy and Great Rome]

And thence he went to embark on the sea. And he saw on the shore of the sea a monastery of the Romans, and there were deposited in their treasury two silver caskets, in one of which was the head of Mar John Chrysostom, in the other that of the Reverend Pope who baptized King Constantine. And he embarked, and got out on the broad sea. And he saw in it a mountain from which all day long smoke ascends and by night fire is exhibited, and none can approach its neighborhood for the smell of the sulphur. For people say that the Great Serpent is there, after whom that sea is called Athlia.[1] For that sea is a terror, [54*] many thousands of men have perished in it. At the end of two months he gained the shore of the sea, after much travail and weariness and discomfort.

And he disembarked at a city called Naples. The name of its King was Irid-shardalo. He had audience with the King and declared to him for what they had come. He received him joyfully and honored him. It happened that there was a quarrel

[9] This tomb, in the Church of the Apostles, according to ancient authorities of porphyry, has now disappeared (Chabot).

[1] This eruption of Aetna witnessed by our traveller is a matter of historical record for June 18; see the next note. 'Athlia,' may be Italia, but the sense of the etymology given is obscure.

between him and another king, whose name was Idar-arcon.   And
the latter's forces came with many ships, and the other's forces
were got ready.   And they met in battle with one another.   And
Idar-arcon conquered King Irid-shardalo, and killed of his opponents
12,000 men, and sank their ships in the sea.   Meanwhile Rabban
Sauma and his companions sat on the top of the roof of the mansion, and they were amazed at the custom of the Franks, that they
killed none apart from the contestants.[2]   [55*] And thence they
went by horse on land.   While they passed through cities and
villages, they were amazed that there was not a region which was
devoid of cultivation.   And on the way he heard that the Reverend
Pope was deceased.[3]

And after some days they reached Great Rome.   And they entered
the Church of Peter and Paul, for the monastery of the See of the
Reverend Pope is there.[4]   And after the death of the Reverend
Pope there were twelve men conducting the See called Cardinals.[5]

[2] *Irid-shardalo* = il ri Charles Do, *i.e.*, King Charles II, of Anjou, son of the turbulent
Charles I, who died 1285; *Idar-arcon* = il ri Aragon, *i.e.*, Jacomo the Aragonese King
of Sicily; that dynasty being the mortal enemy of the House of Anjou.   Chabot
has been able to identify this sea-battle.   It was the engagement fought off the coast
of Naples, more exactly in the Bay of Sorrento on St. John's Day (June 24), 1287,
between the Aragonese admiral Roger dell' Oria and the squadron of the Count of
Artois, protector in Charles II's name and guardian of Charles Martel the young son
of that king, the latter being then a captive in the hands of Peter of Aragon.   The
sharp engagement was won by the Aragonese admiral, who thereupon entered the
city, which had been in his opponent's control and which finally submitted to him.
The identification enables us to fix the date of Bar Sauma's arrival at Naples.   For
the graphic contemporary description of the battle see Muratori, *Rerum italicarum
scriptores* (ed. 1), xiii, 316 (for a translation of this Italian document I am indebted
to my friend Mr. George F. Cole); to which I add further details of the battle from
the *Historia sicula* in the new edition of Muratori, xiii, pt. 3, 100 (Chabot adds some
other sources).   The latter document, p. 97, gives a date for an eruption of Aetna
that greatly disturbed the combatant ships on the coast of Sicily, for June 18; and
this is the eruption Bar Sauma records.   Who the 'king' was whom Sauma saw is
a mystery; *cf.* p. 66*, note 23.

[3] Honorius IV, d. April 3, 1287.

[4] This monastery must be the Vatican.   The names of Peter and Paul are also
given to it below.   It is hardly necessary to remind the reader that the buildings in
question were the ancient ones preceding the grand constructions of the 16th century.
But the actual residence of the Popes till 1305 was St. John Lateran; see Hare, *Walks
in Rome*, 414.

[5] The College of Cardinals was then much depleted.   Similarly at the election
of Celestine V in 1294 there were only twelve Cardinals present; see Gregorovius.
Rome in the Middle Ages, vol. 5, pt. 2, 516.   Gregorovius notes that the meetings

And when they were in council to elect a Pope, Rabban Sauma sent word to them that "we are ambassadors from King Arghon and the Catholicus of the East." Then the Cardinals bade them enter. And the Frank who came in with Rabban Sauma instructed them that when they entered the monastery of the Reverend Pope, there was an altar there which they should worship, and [56*] thence go and salute the Cardinals. And they did so. And as it pleased the Cardinals, when Rabban Sauma entered, none rose in his presence, for it was not the custom of these twelve men to do so because of the dignity of the See. And they sat Rabban Sauma alongside of them. One of them asked him:[6] "How art thou after the toil of travel?" He answered: "By your prayers I am happy and content." And he said to him: "Why hast thou come hither?" He said to him: "The Mongols with the Catholicus of the East have sent me to the Reverend Pope in behalf of Jerusalem. And he has sent letters with me." They said to him: "Content thyself at present, and later we shall speak with one another." And they assigned him quarters and lodged him there.

And after three days the Cardinals sent and called him. And when he came to them, they began to ask him: "What is this region? And why hast thou come?" And he said so and so. [57*] They said to him: "Where does the Catholicus live? And who of the Apostles taught your region?" He answered them: "Mar Thomas and Mar Addai and Mar Mari taught our region, and we hold to the ordinances they gave us until now." They said to him: "Where is the See of the Catholicus?'" He said: "In Baghdad." They responded: "What art thou there?" He answered: "I am the Deacon of the monastery and Master of the students and Visitator-General." They said: "We are surprised that thou art a Christian and a Deacon of the patriarchal See of the East, and yet hast come on an embassy of the King of the Mongols." He said: "Know, my Fathers, that many of our Fathers went to the lands of the Mongols and Turks and Chinese and taught them. And to-day there are many Mongol Christians.

---

of the present electors were held at the late Pope's private villa, so that this assemblage in the Vatican was temporary. The word here used for 'cardinals' is *kaltônârê*, but below *kardânê*.

[6] For the identity of this personage see p. 76*.

Indeed some of the children of the King and Queen [58*] are baptized and confess the Christ. And they have churches with them in the Camp. And they honor the Christians greatly, and there are also many Believers among them. And the King, since he is assiduous in affection for the Catholicus and is desirous to conquer Palestine and the lands of Syria, desires your help because of the captivity of Jerusalem. For this purpose he has chosen and sent me. And since I am a Christian, my word should be credible with you." They said to him: "What is thy creed, and what line of doctrine art thou attached to,—that which the Reverend Pope accepts to-day or another?" He replied: "As for us Orientals none has come to us from the Pope, for the holy Apostles whom I have named taught us, and up to the present we hold fast to what they committed to us." They said to him: "How believest thou? Expound thy creed."

[THE CREED OF RABBAN SAUMA WHICH THE CARDINALS DEMANDED OF HIM]

He answered them: "I believe in one God, hidden, eternal, without beginning and without [59*] end, Father and Son and Holy Spirit, three equal Persons [qenômê], inseparable, in whom there is not a first or second, nor a younger and elder, who are in one Nature [keyânâ] but in three Persons, the Father Begetter, the Son Begotten, the Spirit Proceeding; that at the end of the time one of the Persons of the Royal Trinity, to wit, the Son, clothed Himself with perfect man, Jesus Christ, of the Holy Virgin Mary, and was united with him personally [parsôpâ'ith, from Greek prosopon], and in him redeemed the world; who in His Godhead was eternally of the Father, and in His humanity in time was born of Mary, a unity not to be dissolved nor broken forever, a unity without intermixture or confusion or articulation; and this Son is of a unity, perfect God [60*] and perfect Man, two Natures [keyânê] and two Persons [qenômê], one Personality [parsôpâ]."[1]

---

[1] There is no definite liturgical formula of creed in the Nestorian Church as in the western Churches. Various credal statements, of which the above is a sample, abound; some such are given by Assemani, iii, pt. 2, c. 7; Badger, vol. 2, c. 6; Renaudot, *Orien-*

They said to him: "The Holy Spirit, does He proceed from the Father [alone] or from the Son [also]?"[2] He answered: "The Father and the Son and the Holy Spirit, are They associated or separated in regard to Nature?" They replied: "They are associated in Nature but separated in Individualities [dîlâyâthâ]." He said: "What are Their Individualities?" They say: "The Father's is the quality of Begetter, the Son's that of being Begotten, the Spirit's that of Proceeding." He said: "Which of Them is the cause of the other?" They said: "The Father is cause of the Son, and the Son is cause of the Spirit." He said: "If They are equal in the matter of Nature and operation and power and authority, and They are just Three Persons, how can one of Them be cause of the other? Then the inference would be [61*] that the Spirit is cause of something else. But the subject-matter is ultimately for the confession of wise men only. Further we cannot follow a demonstration agreeing with this argument of yours. For the soul is cause of reason and life, but reason is not the cause of life. And the orb of the sun is cause of glow and heat, but heat is not the cause of the glow. So again we are disposed to think that the Father must be cause of the Son and the Spirit, and They two His causations. Adam begat Sheth and produced Eve, and they are three in the matter of begetting and bringing forth, but not distinguished at all in the matter of humanity." They said: "We confess that the Spirit proceeds from the Father and the Son; we have not, as we have said, attempted a trial of thy modesty." He said: "It is not true that to any one thing there are two causes, or three or four, but I think this is not like our confession." And they terminated [62*] his discourse with many arguments. But they honored him for his discourse.

talische Liturgien, end of vol. 2, and one of date 612 by Giamil, in Oriens christianus, 1, 61 et seq.; and especially a large list in W. A. Wigram, The Assyrian Church, S. P. C. K., 1910, c. 13, 'Official Christology of the Assyrian Church,' with extensive discussion. For critical discussion of the Nestorian Creed see Kattenbusch, Das apostolische Symbol, 1, 245–248.

[2] The Cardinals naturally proceed to examine him on the burning dogmatic issue between East and West, the filioque addition to the Western Creed. The following discussion is of interest, and exhibits the dialectic ability of the Nestorian advocate. A memorandum of the discussion may well have been made, and there is no reason to think with some critics that this is a bit of dogmatic padding. The text adds au pertshê, 'or the separated ones,' which I cannot explain.

Then he said to them: "I have come from far lands not to dispute nor to expound the themes of the Faith; but to receive a benediction from the Reverend Pope and the shrines of the saints have I come, and to declare the business of the King and the Catholicus. If it be agreeable to you that we leave the discussion and you make arrangement and appoint some one who will show me the churches here and the shrines of the saints, you will confer a great favor upon your servant and disciple." Then they called the governor of the city and certain monks and ordered them to show him the churches and the places of the saints there. And so they went forth at once, and they saw the places which we will now record.

First, they went into the Church of Peter and Paul. Now beneath the throne [tribune] is a chapel, and there is deposited [63*] the body of St. Peter.[3] And above the throne is the altar; and the altar which is in that great temple has four gates, and at each gate carved doors of iron. And on the altar the Reverend Pope consecrates [celebrates the Eucharist], and none but he presides at the service of that altar.[4] And afterwards they saw that throne of Mar Peter,[5] on which they seat the Reverend Pope when they consecrate him. And further they saw the pure piece of garment in which Our Lord left His portrait, sending it to King Abgar of Edessa.[6] But the majesty of that church and its glory cannot be told. It stands on 108 pillars.[7] And

---

[3] The Sepulchral Chapel under the present high altar and dome, where is the sarcophagus of St. Peter.

[4] This privilege still obtains.

[5] Probably the ancient wooden chair of St. Peter, now encased in Bernini's Cathedra Petri in the Tribune; see Hare, *Walks in Rome*, 517, for the earlier locations of this chair.

[6] The Syriac *Doctrine of Addai* tells how Abgar's messenger to the Lord painted the Lord's picture for his master. Ultimately (*e.g.*, in Cedrenus) this legend was magnified into the story of a veil on which the Lord left the impress of his features. This relic was later taken from Edessa to Byzantium. The writer appears to confuse the Oriental legend with the story of St. Veronica's veil, still a relic in St. Peter's, where it is exhibited publicly at the end of Holy Week; see Hare pp. 511 *et seq.*, and Marucchi *Basiliques et églises de Rome*, 123. Polo, describing the 'salamander cloth' (asbestos) made by the Chinese (i, c. 42), relates: "I may add that they have at Rome a napkin of this stuff, which the Grand Kaan sent to the Pope to make a wrapper for the Holy Sudarium of Jesus Christ." And Yule adds that such an asbestos cloth is still preserved in the Vatican.

[7] *Cf.* the 360 gates (or pillars) attributed by the writer to Santa Sophia. The

there is in it another altar at which their King of Kings receives ordination—and he is called Emperor King of Kings—from the Pope. For they say that after the service ['prayers'] the Reverend Pope takes the crown with his feet and invests him, [64*] and *he* [the Pope] puts it [the crown] on his head,—so that the priesthood may dominate over royalty, they say.[8]

And after they had seen all the churches and monasteries in Great Rome, they went out of the city to the Church of Mar Paul the Apostle; for his tomb is also beneath the altar, and the chain with which Paul was bound, having been brought there, is there.[9] Also there is deposited in that altar a casket of gold in which is placed the head of the Martyr Stephen and the hand of Mar Ananias who baptized Paul. Also the staff of the Apostle Paul is there. Thence they went to the place where the Apostle Paul was crowned [with martyrdom]. And they say that when his head was cut off, it leaped up three times, and each time it called "Christ, Christ," and from the three places where it fell there issued water at each place and it is good for cures and relief of all who are afflicted.[10] And there is a great church [*nausâ*, lit. 'nave'] there,[11] [65*] and in it the bones of illustrious martyrs and fathers; and they received benediction from them. Further, they went to the Church of the Lady Mary,[12]

figure may include the colonnade of the old church in front and the portico connecting with the city; see Marucchi, p. 119.

[8] Marucchi, pp. 59 *et seq.*, gives at length an eye-witness's account of the coronation of Frederick III in 1452, and extracts from one of the appropriate rituals of the 14th or 15th century. The investment occurred at the altar of St. Maurice. The reference to the Pope's feet is obscure. The new emperor kissed the Pope's feet at the beginning and the end of the ceremonies. This abasement of royalty must have been passing strange in the Oriental's eyes.

[9] St. Paul's Without the Walls; the ancient church was destroyed by fire in 1823. The new church still boasts the tomb of St. Paul.

[10] These three springs, where the same tradition survives, beyond St. Paul's, are contained in the present Church of San Paolo alle Tre Fontane (16th century); it is one of three churches at the place, including the ancient one mentioned next.

[11] The ancient Church of SS. Vincenzio and Anastasio, of the 7th century, restored in 1221; still practically the very building our pilgrim saw. Hare remarks, p. 614, "There is no church in Rome which breathes a greater air of antiquity than here." Anastasius was an Oriental martyr.

[12] S. Maria Maggiore; the nave dates from the 5th century. Nicholas IV, who was elected during our pilgrim's visit, redecorated the church.

and that of Mar John Baptist.[13]   And they saw in it [the latter] the coat of Our Lord which was not sewn.   And there is in this church the table upon which Our Lord consecrated the Eucharist and gave it to His disciples.[14]   And every year the Reverend Pope celebrates the Mysteries of Passover [Maundy-Thursday] on this table.[15]   And there are in this church four pillars of brass, the thickness of each six cubits, which they say the Kings brought from Jerusalem.[16]   And they saw there the font in which King Constantine the Conqueror was baptized, of dark [black] polished stone.[17]   The pillars of this church are 140 in number, of white marble, for the church is large and wide.   They saw the place where Simon Cephas argued with Simon, in which the latter fell and his bones were broken.[18]   Thence they went to the Church of the Lady Mary.[19]   And they brought out to them the casket of crystal [beryl] in which [66*] is the garment of the Lady Mary, and the piece of wood on which Our Lord slept when He was a child.[20]   And they saw the head of the Apostle Matthew in a casket

[13] The Church of St. John Lateran; the present church dates from the 14th century.

[14] The *Handbook to Christian and Ecclesiastical Rome* (see note 6 at p. 78*) notes that on Maundy-Thursday the table on which it is supposed the Last Supper was celebrated is also shown. "This is above the altar of the Holy Sacrament, in the left transept, behind glass, and candles are lighted there. . . . The Table is of cedar wood." Marucchi simply records, p. 85, that the relic of the Table was preserved there; while Hare, p. 403, knows only of the wooden table, still preserved in the Lateran, on which St. Peter is said to have celebrated Mass in the house of Pudens. Thus authorities differ!

[15] The Holy Week Ceremonies are fully described later, pp. 78* *seq.*

[16] *Cf.* Hare, p. 405: "The altar of the Sacrament has four grand fluted bronze columns, said to have been brought from Jerusalem by Titus, and to be hollow and filled with earth from Palestine." He adds that these columns are recorded in a 13th century list of Lateran relics.

[17] This font, an ancient bath of green basalt, is in the antique Baptistry outside the church.

[18] The local tradition is that Simon Magus in his dispute with St. Peter attempted to fly in proof of his magic, but fell and was dashed in pieces. See Chabot, who cites from the 'Ordo romanus,' in Mabillon, *Museum italicum*, 2, 143, which assigns the exact spot of the catastrophe: "Progrediens inter forum Trajani et forum Caesaris subintrat arcum Nerviae [*sic*] inter templum ejusdem deae et templum Jani, ascendit ante asylum per silicem ubi cecidit Simon Magus iuxta templum Romuli."

[19] See note 12.

[20] Five boards of the Cradle, the Santa Culla, are shown in the church in the Confession of St. Matthew.

of silver.[21]   Also they saw the foot of the Apostle Philip and the arm
of James the son of Zebedee in the Church of the Apostles there.[22]
And after this they saw buildings which word of speech cannot
relate, and the narrative concerning the buildings would cause a
prolongation of the story in any attempt to relate them, therefore
I will excuse myself.

Afterwards Rabban Sauma and his companions returned to the
Cardinals, and he made his acknowledgments that they had deemed
him worthy of the sight of those sanctuaries and of the benedictions
that come from them.   And Rabban Sauma asked leave of them
to go to the King in Rome.[23]   And they said: "We cannot give
you a reply [to your commission] until a Pope is in office."

And thence they went to the land of Tuszekan [Tuscany?],
and were given honors.   And from there [67*] they came to Genoa.
Now there is no king in that place, but the people institute as chief
over it for the government one whom they desire.[24]   When they
heard that an ambassador of King Arghon had arrived, the Chief
went out with all the crowd and brought them into the city with
honor.   And there was there a great church with the name of
Senalornia the Saint.[25]   And in it was the holy body of Mar John
Baptist in a casket of pure silver.[26]   And they saw also a bowl
of six-sided [sic] emeralds, and those people told them that this is
that in which Our Lord and His disciples ate the Passover, and
when Jerusalem was taken it was brought here.[27]   And thence

[21] Still shown in the church.

[22] These last two relics refer us to the Church of the Holy Apostles, dedicated to
SS. Philip and James; our pilgrim saw the structure dating to the 5th century, mod-
ernized after the pilgrim's day.   The relics of the two apostles were rediscovered in
1873; Marucchi, p. 105.

[23] There evidently follows a lacuna in the narrative.   Probably they discovered
to their surprise that there was no king in Rome, and indeed no emperor, at least to
Roman eyes.   The nearest approach to such a personage was Charles II of Anjou,
now a prisoner of Peter of Aragon, or his minor son Charles Martel; see p. 54*, note,
and cf. p. 75*.

[24] This was previous to the establishment of the dogeship in 1339.

[25] The Duomo di San Lorenzo, built in the 12th century, restored in the 14th.

[26] The present silver shrine dates from 1437; Hare, *Cities of Northern and Central
Italy*, 1, 38.

[27] This is the 'Holy Grail,' brought from Cæsarea to Genoa in 1101, and reverenced
as the glory of the city.   It is an octagonal bowl, long regarded as an emerald, but
now known to be ancient glass.   It was looted by the French in 1809, and was broken
on its return in 1815; Hare, *ib.* 38.

they came to the land of Onbar.[28] And the people there saw that they were not fasting on the first Saturday ['sabbath'] of the Fast [Lent]. And when they asked them, "Why do you so, and separate yourselves from all Christians?", [68*] they answered: "This is our custom. When we were first instructed, our ancestors were weak in faith and were not able to fast; their teachers bade them to fast forty days."[29]

[RABBAN SAUMA IN FRANCE]

And after this they went to the land of Paris to King Francis.[1] And the King sent out many people to meet them, and they brought them into the city with honor and great acclaim. Now his lands extended for a month's length and more. And he assigned them a lodging place. And after three days King Francis sent an officer to Rabban Sauma and summoned him. And when he came in he rose up before him and honored him, and he said to him: "For what hast thou come, and who sent thee?" He said to him: "King Arghon and the Catholicus of the East have sent me on behalf of Jerusalem." And he declared to him all that [69*] he knew, and gave him the letters he had with him, and the presents, i.e., the gifts, which he brought. King Francis answered him: "If the Mongols, although they are not Christians, are fighting with the Arabs because of the captivity of Jerusalem, it still more behooves us to fight and go forth in force, if Our Lord will." Rabban Sauma said to him: "Now that we have seen your praiseworthy majesty and have viewed the glory of your power with the eye of flesh, we ask of you that you give orders that the citizens show us the churches and the shrines and the relics of the saints, and all that is to be found with you and not anywhere else, so that

[28] Probably Lombardy (Bedjan).

[29] The narrative of the incident must be proleptical of the second visit to Genoa, when Sauma was there in Lent. The Latin criticism of the Nestorians is due to the fact that the latter were strictly forbidden under severe canonical penalty from fasting on Saturdays as well as on Sundays, with the exception of Easter Even; see Assemani, iii, pt. 2, 705 et seq. The Nestorian Calendar had seven Sundays before Easter, preceded with the Fast of Jonah, and in this way they may have counted forty days.

[1] 'François' was understood as 'Francis' instead of 'French.' The King was Philip IV. Similarly Bar Hebræus, Chron. syr., 484, calls Louis IX Redafrans.

when we return we can tell and declare in the lands what we have
seen." Then the King gave orders to his officers to "go and show
them all the marvels which we have, and afterwards I will show
them what I have." And so those officials went out with
them. [70*] And they remained a full month in that great city of
Paris, and saw everything in it.

Now there are there 30,000 students, who study in ecclesiastical
subjects, that is Interpretation [nuhhârâ, 'illumination'], and in
subjects outside of this: the Exegesis, that is Interpretation, of
all the Holy Scriptures, and Wisdom, that is Philosophy (philasoph-
utha), and Rhetoric, along with Medicine and Geometry and
Arithmetic and the science of the planets and stars, which they
are very assiduous to write up. And they all receive stipends from
the King. Further, they saw a great church where the coffins of
the Kings lie.[2] And their effigies in gold and silver are upon
their tombs. And there are in the service of the tombs of those
Kings five hundred monks who eat and drink at the King's cost,
and they are diligent in fast and prayer at the tombs of those Kings.
And the crowns and arms of these Kings [71*] along with their
clothing are alongside these tombs. In fine, they saw everything
worthy of praise and honor.

Afterwards the King sent and called them, and they came to
him at the church.[3] And they saw him standing by the altar
and they greeted him. And he asked Rabban Sauma: "Now
you have seen what we have, does there remain anything else
beside?" Then he made his acknowledgments. And forthwith
he went up with the King to an upper chamber of gold, which the
King opened. And he brought out of it a casket of crystal ['beryl'],
in which was set the Crown of Thorns, which the Jews set upon
the head of Our Lord when they crucified Him. And the Crown
was visible in the casket before it was opened, because of the
translucency of the crystal. And further there was in it a relic

---

[2] The Church of St. Denis, near Paris, the burial-place of the French kings; the
pilgrim saw the church as beautified by St. Louis.

[3] Sainte Chapelle, on the Ile de France, built by St. Louis in 1245–1248 to house
the Crown of Thorns and other precious relics, which he brought back with him
from the Eighth Crusade. Along with the Crown are a fragment of the Cross and
a nail from it. The Chapel proper is on the upper floor. The relics are now in the
Treasury of Notre-Dame.

of the Wood of the Cross.   And the King said to them that "when our ancestors took Constantinople [4] and despoiled Jerusalem, they brought these benedictions from there."   And we blessed the King. Then we persuaded him to give us orders to leave.[5] [72*] Then he said to us: "I will send with you one of the great officers at my side to give King Arghon a reply."   And he gave him gifts and fine garments.

[RABBAN SAUMA GOES TO THE KING OF ENGELTERRA]

And they went thence, that is, from Paris, to the King Ilnagtar to Kesonia.[1]   And when after twenty days they reached their city, the citizens went out to meet them, and asked them: "Who are you?"   They answered them: "We are ambassadors, and from beyond the Eastern Seas have we come.   We are delegates of the King and the Patriarch, to wit, of the King of the Mongols." And the people went quickly to the King and informed him, and he received them with delight, and he brought them into his court. Then the party of Rabban Sauma forthwith gave him the dispatches of King Arghon and the presents he sent him, along with the document which Mar Catholicus [73*] gave him.   And he was greatly delighted.   And when discourse arose about the business of Jerusalem, his joy was still more increased.   And he said: "We Kings of these cities carry the cross as a sign on our bodies, and we have no thought apart from this business.   And my mind is gratified when I hear that somewhat of what I have thought of King Arghon has planned."[2]   And he commanded Rabban Sauma to celebrate the Eucharist ['consecrate the Offering'], and he cele-

[4] A casual allusion to the outrageous despoliation of Constantinople by the Fourth Crusade in 1204, when the French and the Venetians divided the loot.

[5] The first person of the original diary slips in here.

[1] 'Ilnagtar' is corruption of 'Angleterre,' and 'Kesonia' of 'Gascony.' As is well known, Edward I of England was then in his French province of Aquitaine-Gascony, spending three years there from the Spring of 1286 to August, 1289; see, e.g., *Annales londonienses*, in the Rolls Series, *Chronicles of the Reigns of Edward I and Edward II*, pp. 95, 97.   Cordier, in his edition of Yule, *Cathay*, 1, 166, and Mingana, *Early Spread of Christianity*, 314, wrongly hold that Sauma reached London.   But the latter thought he was in England.

[2] Oddly enough there is no reference to the Palestinian Crusade of Edward, before his accession, 1269-71.

brated the laudable Mysteries, the King and his courtiers attending, and the King received the Communion ['the *sacrum*']. And on the same day the King gave a great banquet. Then Rabban Sauma said "We desire, O King, that whatever there is in this country of churches and shrines thou wouldst have shown to us, that when we return to the Orientals we may tell the story." He answered: "So shall you say to King Arghon and all the Orientals, that we have seen something, and that there is nothing more admirable than this, namely, that in the lands of the Franks there are not two creeds, but only one, that which confesses Jesus Christ, and they are all Christians." And he gave us many gifts and our expenses.[3]

[74*] [RABBAN SAUMA RETURNS TO ROME]

And thence we went to winter in the city of Genoa. And when we arrived there we saw a garden like Paradise, where the winter is not cold, nor the summer hot, and where green vegetation is found all the year long, and trees which do not shed their leaves nor are without fruits. There is there one kind of vine that bears seven crops in the year, but wine is not pressed from the grapes.

At the end of the winter there came from the country of Almadan a distinguished man who was the Visitator of the Reverend Pope, going to Rome.[1] And when he heard that Rabban Sauma was there, he came to greet him. And when he entered, they exchanged greetings and kissed one another in Christian love. And he said to Rabban Sauma: [75*] "I have come to see thee, for I have heard of thee that thou art a good and wise man, and also that thou desirest to go to Rome." Rabban Sauma said to him: "What can I say to thee, honored friend? For I have come on an embassy from King Arghon and the Catholicus of the East in behalf of Jerusalem to the Reverend Pope, and it is a full year

---

[3] For the subsequent correspondence of Edward with the Mongols, see Int. § ii.

[1] 'Almadan,' *i.e.*, Germany; he heard 'allemand.' Chabot interestingly identifies this personage as the Cardinal-Legate Jean de Tusculum, citing Mansi, *Coll. concil.*, 24, 943, Baronius, *Annales, anno* 1287. This Cardinal had been sent to Germany at the end of 1286 to negotiate for the coronation of Rudolph of Hapsburg, and he presided at an unsuccessful council at Würzburg, March 18, 1287.

that I have been here, and a Pope is not seated. What shall I go
and say and answer to the Mongols? They, whose heart is harder
than rock, desire to take the Holy City, while those whose
business it is do not resolve upon it, even do not think of the thing
at all. We know not what we shall go and say." The Visitator
said to him: "Thy words are true. I will go myself, and all the
words thou hast spoken I will tell literally to the Cardinals, and I
will constrain them to elect a Pope."

And the Visitator departed and came to Rome, and told it to
the King,[2] and he to the Reverend Pope. [76*] On that same day
he sent a messenger to them, that the party of Rabban Sauma
should come. And they on the arrival of the messenger diligently
set out for Rome, and they reached it in fifteen days.[3] And they
asked: "Who is this Pope they have elected?" They answered
him: "It is the bishop who conversed with you, when you came
here first, his name is Nicholas."[4] And they rejoiced greatly.
When they arrived, the Reverend Pope sent people to meet them,
the Metropolitan along with many others. And Rabban Sauma
went in at once to the Reverend Pope. And he was seated on his
throne. And he [Bar Sauma] presented himself with homage and
kissed his feet and hands. And he retired backwards [lit. 'turned
back'] with his hands clasped. And he said to the Reverend Pope:
"May thy throne be established, O Father, forever, and blessed
may it be above all kings and peoples, and may peace reign in thy
days in the whole Church [77*] to the ends of the earth! Now that
I have seen thy face it has brightened my eyes that I do not come
heartbroken to the lands. I acknowledge the grace of God that
He has counted me worthy of the sight of thee." And he presented
to him the gift of King Arghon along with his letters and also the

[2] The reference to a king appears gratuitous; cf. at p. 66*. Charles II was not
released until November, 1288; he was crowned by the Pope the following May (Gregorovius, *Rome in the Middle Ages*, vol. 5, pt. 2, 510).

[3] This statement is proleptic to the following inquiry.

[4] Nicholas IV, Jerome of Ascoli, consecrated February 22, 1288. He was the first
Franciscan to become Pope, had distinguished himself as a Legate to the East and
was titular Patriarch of Byzantium; he was deeply concerned in a Crusade (Gregorovius, p. 507 *et seq.*). Hence the interest shown by him from the very first in this
Oriental embassy, p. 56*, and further expressed in the following narrative. He was
an extremist in orthodoxy, and it was he who as Minister-general in 1277 sentenced
Roger Bacon to prison for his errors.

gift of Mar Yaballaha the Catholicus, that is, 'the blessing,' and his letters. And the Reverend Pope was glad and rejoiced, and he honored Rabban Sauma more than was wont. And he said to him: "It will be well if thou celebrate the season with us and see our custom,"—for that day was the middle of the Dominical Fast [Lent]. He replied: "Your command is high and lofty." And the Reverend Pope assigned an abode for his sojourn, and appointed attendants to give him all he desired.

And after some days Rabban Sauma said to the Reverend Pope: "I desire to consecrate [the Eucharist] that you too may see our custom." And he bade him to consecrate, as he requested. And on that day a great congregation assembled to see how [78*] the ambassador of the Mongols consecrates. And when they saw, they rejoiced and said: "The language is different, but the rite is one." Now that same day when he consecrated was the Sunday of 'Who is the Healer?'[5] And when he had solemnized the Mysteries, he went in to the Reverend Pope and greeted him. And he said to Rabban Sauma: "May God receive thy offering and bless thee and pardon thy faults and sins!" And Rabban Sauma said: "With the pardon of my faults and sins which I have received from thee, O Father, I desire of thy fatherliness, O Holy Father, that I may receive the Communion from thy hands, so that I may have complete forgiveness." And he said: "It shall be so."

And when Sunday came again, that is, Hosanna Sunday [Palm Sunday], there assembled in the morning thousands and tens of thousands without number before the throne [of the Pope], and they brought olive branches.[6] And he blessed them; he gave the

---

[5] *I.e.*, the Fifth Sunday in Lent, as the following shows. Sundays were often known after their Proper Anthems or Antiphons, as in old Latin usage.

[6] The present practice places the chief Palm Sunday service at St. Peter's. But the Lateran is still the traditional 'Station' for that day in Holy Week; and doubtless it was that church in which the present service was held. For the ceremonies of Holy Week, so fully described in this Biography, I have consulted especially the *Handbook to Christian and Ecclesiastical Rome*, pt. ii, *The Liturgy in Rome*, by H. M. and M. A. R. T., London, 1897, a valuable volume now out of print, a copy of which has been kindly lent me by my friend and colleague, Prof. J. Cullen Ayer. At the end of that volume is given a calendar of the services for Holy Week and Easter. The name Hosanna Sunday is also given in Roman use to Palm Sunday. The Benediction of the Palms on that day is still an elaborate ceremony, the Pope blessing special palms; see the *Handbook*, c. 7.

blessing to the Cardinals, and then to the Metropolitans, and then to the Bishops, and then to the officials, and then he shed it on all the people. And he arose from the throne, [79*] and with rejoicing they brought him to the church. And he entered the chancel and changed his vestments and put on the crimson garments of the rite, which were embroidered with gold and gems and hyacinths and pearls, down to the shoes of his feet, that is, his sandals. And he entered the sanctuary ['altar'], and came to the pulpit, and he preached and exhorted the people. And he consecrated the Mysteries. And he gave Rabban Saumà the Communion first, after he had confessed his sinfulness. And he absolved him from his faults and sins and those of his ancestors. And he rejoiced greatly to receive Communion from the hand of the Reverend Pope, and he received the Communion with tears and weeping, acknowledging the grace of God and thinking upon the mercy poured out upon him.

And afterwards on Holy Passover [Maundy-Thursday] the Reverend Pope came to the Church of St. John Baptist,[7] after a great congregation had assembled, and he went up to the great upper room there, all furnished and decorated.[8] Before the room was a great lobby. And there went in with him the Cardinals and Metropolitans and Bishops. And they began [80*] with service; and when it was finished, the Reverend Pope made an allocution and preached to the people, as was the custom. And there was not a sound heard from the multitude of people, except for the 'Amen'; and when 'Amen' was said, the earth trembled from their cries.[9] Thence he went down to the front of the altar and made a quantity of chrism oil, that, is, oil of anointing.[10] And

[7] St. John Lateran, v. sup., p. 65*. The 'Station' of the day is still the Lateran.

[8] Probably the very sacred and ancient upper chapel, the Sancta Sanctorum, which is reserved with slight exception to the Pope's person alone; Hare, *Walks in Rome*, 412.

[9] This ancient ceremony is vouched for in the *Handbook*, pp. 292 *et seq.*: "The Pope used to impart a solemn benediction from the external loggia of S. Peter's [the Lateran's successor] after the mass on Holy Thursday. This is a relic of the solemn reconciliation and benediction of penitents which used to take place on that day." And there is given a striking parallelism to the present account of the silence of the multitude: "Those who have witnessed the Benediction say that in that vast gathering of people one 'could hear a pin drop' as the Pope imparted his blessing."

[10] "In the Basilicas of S. Peter and the Lateran, during the Mass of this morning

afterwards he consecrated the Atoning Mysteries, and gave Communion to the people.   And he went forth thence and came into the great nave.   And he distributed and gave to the holy fathers to each one two leaves of gold and thirty sheets [?] of silver.   And he departed.   And the Reverend Pope assembled the monks of his monastery, and he washed their feet, and wiped them with a cloth that was girt about his loins, to the last.[11]   And when the full rite of Passover was accomplished, at noon he gave a great dinner.   And the servants set before each man his portion of food. And those who sat there were two thousand more or less.   And when they removed the food, there remained [but] three hours of the day.[12]

[81*] And on the next day, which was the Passion of Our Redeemer [Good Friday], the Reverend Pope put on a black cassock, and all the clergy likewise; and they went out barefoot, and came to the Church of the Adorable Cross.[13]   And the Reverend Pope worshipped and kissed it [the Cross], and he gave it to each one of the clergy.   And when the crowd saw it, they uncovered their heads and kneeled on their knees and worshipped it.   And he preached and discoursed to the people.   And

(Holy Thursday) is performed the Rite of Benediction of the oil of catechumens, and of the oil of the sick, and the confection of the chrism"; so the *Handbook*, p. 264, which also gives the order of the services.   It is similarly the day for that purpose throughout the Latin world.

[11] According to Hare, p. 413, this was the practice as long as the Lateran palace was inhabited, down to 1580; the feet of twelve priests or poor men were washed by the Pope on Maundy-Thursday.   This custom is now celebrated by the Pope at St. Peter's.   See further, the *Handbook*, 251.

[12] This banquet hall is doubtless the ancient Triclinium, the great dining chamber of the Popes, used particularly at Christmas, Easter and imperial coronations; see Marucchi, p. 105.   Hare, p. 410, records that its terminal apse survives, but Marucchi holds that nothing remains of it.

[13] The church is Santa Croce in Gerusalemme, which boasts possession of the Title of the Holy Cross.   The pilgrim saw the church of the 12th century, of which little remains.   It was consecrated to the Passion of the Lord, as S. Mary Maggiore to his Nativity and Resurrection, the Lateran to his Ascension.   The solemn offices of Good Friday used to be celebrated there, attended by the Pope, Cardinals and a vast throng; see Marucchi, p. 347.   It is still the Station for Good Friday, and the ceremonial is more impressive there on that day than in any other church in Rome; Hare, p. 423 *et seq.*   And this custom of the barefoot procession is corroborated by the *Handbook*, 294: "On Good Friday the Pope and Cardinals went first to the Sancta Sanctorum chapel in the Lateran, and thence the Pope walked barefoot to S. Croce, all reciting Psalms."   In the Latin Rite the vestments for the day are all black.

when the Cross had turned around in the four directions, and when service was finished, he brought some of the Host ['Offering'] of the Passover [Maundy-Thursday] and put wine with it. And the Reverend Pope received the Communion alone, for it is not the custom for Christians to offer the Offering on the day of the Passion of Our Redeemer.[14] Then he returned to his monastery.

And on the day of the Sabbath of Light [15] the Pope went to the church, and they read the books of the Prophets and the Prophecies about the Christ.[16] And they placed a font and set about it branches of myrtle. And the Reverend Pope consecrated the baptismal water himself, and he baptized three children and signed them [with the sign of the cross].[17] And he entered the chancel, and he put off his vestments of the Passion, [82*] and put on the robes of his function, the value of which passes telling. And he consecrated the Mysteries.

And on the Sunday of the Resurrection [Easter Day] the Reverend Pope entered the holy Church of the Lady Mary. And they greeted one another, he and the Cardinals and the Metropolitans and the Bishops and the crowds; and they kissed one another on the mouth. And he celebrated the Mysteries, and they received the Communion. And he entered the monastery and he made a great feast and celebration without stint.[18] And on New Sunday [Low Sunday] the Reverend Pope held an Ordination, and he ordained three bishops.[19] And Rabban Sauma's party saw their ritual. And they celebrated the blessed Feasts with them.

14 *I.e.*, the Latin custom of the Mass of the Presanctified.
15 Easter Even; also called the Great Sabbath, as in the Latin Rite *Sabbatum magnum*.
16 According to the *Handbook*, 280, there are still read twelve prophecies, the chanting of which occupies an hour.
17 The monastery and church are those of the Lateran, which is still the Station for the day, and where the principal function is celebrated. The ancient Baptistry was once used on Easter Even for the (compulsory) baptism of a number of Jews, the custom still surviving, according to Hare, p. 401, with neophytes called Jews. The solemn service is still maintained; see the *Handbook*, pp. 280 *et seq.*, which states simply that baptism is performed if candidates are presented.
18 S. Mary Maggiore is still the Station for the day, but the Pontifical Easter services are now at St. Peter's. The banquet was doubtless held in the Lateran Triclinium. Easter Day fell in 1288 on March 28.
19 This was not a regular service for Ordination, which service regularly falls in a season of fasting, *e.g.*, Easter Even or the Embertides; see the *Handbook*, 173. The

And when all this had taken place, he desired of the Reverend Pope permission to depart.   But he said to him: "It is our desire that thou remain with us, and thou shalt be in our company, and we will keep thee as the apple of our eye."   But Rabban Sauma replied: "I, O Father, have come on an embassy to do you service. If my coming were of my own desire, in the outer gate [83*] of your monastery would I accomplish the days of this my life of vanity in your service.   But when I return I will declare to the Kings there the favors you have done to my weakness.   I think it will be a great satisfaction to the Christians.   But I desire of your Holiness that you give me an alms of some of the relics you have."   The Reverend Pope said: "If it were our custom to give everyone these relics, although they were mountains high, they would soon be finished off by the myriads.   But since thou hast come from a far country, we will give thee a few."   And he gave him a small relic from the garment of Our Lord Christ, and from the *poikile* or bonnet of the Lady Mary, and small relics of the saints there.   And he sent to Mar Yaballaha a crown of pure gold for his head, adorned with very precious stones, and clothing for the vestments of his function, red and embroidered with gold, and shoes sewn with small pearls, and boots, [84*] and also a ring from his own finger; and letters patent which contained authorization of his Patriarchate over all the Orientals.   And to Rabban Sauma he gave letters patent as Visitator over all Christians.[20]   And he blessed him.   And he allotted to him for the expenses of his journey 1500 pounds[21] of red gold.   And to King Arghon he sent some gifts.   And he embraced and kissed Rabban Sauma and dismissed him.   And Rabban Sauma rendered thanks to Our Lord that He had deemed him worthy of such boons.

name ' New Sunday ' for the First Sunday after Easter is found in the Armenian rite, s. Neale, *Hist. of the Holy East. Ch.*, 735; it is not recorded in Assemani's Nestorian Calendar.

[20] The letters to these ecclesiastics have not been preserved; for the other correspondence see Int., § ii.

[21] See note at p. 48*.

[CONCERNING THE RETURN OF RABBAN SAUMA FROM ROME FROM
    THE REVEREND POPE CATHOLICUS AND PATRIARCH OF THE
    ROMANS AND OF ALL THE OCCIDENTALS]

And again he crossed the seas from whither he had gone. And
he arrived [85*] safely at King Arghon's in soundness of body and
preservation of soul.   And he gave him the documents of blessing
along with the presents which he brought from the Reverend Pope
as well as from all the Kings of the Franks. And he told him how
they had received him with love, and had warmly listened to the
dispatches he brought.   And he narrated the marvels he had seen
and the might of the empire. And King Arghon rejoiced and was
delighted, and he thanked him and said to him: "We have put
thee to great trouble, seeing thou art an old man.   Therefore we
will not let thee be separated from us.   But we will establish a
church in our royal court ['gate'], and thou shalt serve and pray
in it." Rabban Sauma said: "If Milord the King will command,
let Mar Yaballaha the Catholicus come and receive the gifts which
the Reverend Pope has sent him and the articles for divine worship
which he has donated to him, and he shall be the institutor of the
church which the King establishes in the royal court, and he shall
consecrate it."   And these things came to pass just so.

And since it was not our purpose to relate and compose the
things which Rabban Sauma did and saw, [86*] we have somewhat
abbreviated what he himself wrote in Persian. And these things
which are here recorded have been added and abbreviated in
proportion to the aim of the undertaking.

[THE BENEFACTIONS OF KING ARGHON AND HIS DEATH]

In the year 1598 of the Greek Era [1] King Arghon further gave
orders and brought Mar Yaballaha to the Camp,[2] as Rabban

_____

[1] Chabot corrects to 1599 = 1288 A.D., the year of Sauma's return. But on the
uncertainty of the calculation of the Seleucide era see Mingana's remarks, *Bulletin*
of the John Rylands Library, 1925, 331. He notes that the beginning of the era
may be taken anywhere between 309 and 313 B.C., and that it is generally unsafe to
depend upon the usual addition of 311 years to the Christian era.

[2] For its location see at p. 35*.

Sauma requested.   And because of the honor of the Catholicus and also in order to encourage all the Christians who believed in the Christ and to increase His love among them, he [the King] established a church at the gate of the throne, hard by, so that the ropes of the tent-cloths [87*] of the church were intercrossed with those of his [the King's] house [tent].   And he made a great banquet for three days.   King Arghon himself presented the food and the cup to the Catholicus and so to all his staff ['sons of his service'], although the bishops and the holy fathers and the priests and the deacons and the monks were occupied in the vigils and the [divine] service.[3]   And the King provided that the church should not fail for the sound of a gong.[4]   And thus the praise of the Oriental and Occidental Christians increased until they cried with one voice: "Blessed is the Lord who has enriched us.   And the Lord has visited His people and given it salvation."   And when the Camp moved on, the priests moved the church and all that was in it.   And Rabban Sauma was director of the church and overseer and steward of the stipends of the priests and deacons and visitators and the caretakers of the church.   For King Arghon, for the great love he had for him, commanded that the [Eucharistic] Offering for himself and prayer on his behalf should not cease.

[88*] And at the turn of the year, that is, 1599 [error for 1600] of the Greek Era, in the month Elul [A.D. 1289, September] King Arghon went to the monastery of the city Maragha to see the Reverend Catholicus.   In the month Ab [August] he had his son baptized, and he ordered him to receive the Atoning Mysteries. And so the preaching of Life [5] increased, and the Gospel of the Kingdom of Heaven waxed in all the earth, until that from all sides

[3] In the old days the all-night vigils played a great part in the Nestorian liturgy, and this prevented most of the clergy from attending the banquet.   For these vigils see Assemani, iii, pt. 2, 820.   For the extreme act of courtesy on the King's part cf. the statements made in the Arabic biography cited at end of Int., § iv.

[4] Syriac nâqôshâ, a long piece of wood which is struck with a flexible stick, still the means of announcing the services among the Nestorians.   See Payne-Smith, Thesaurus, 2366, and for the early Arabic references Cheiko, Le christianisme et la littérature chrétienne, Beyrouth, 1912, seq. (Arabic text), 208; also Gottheil, Journal of the American Oriental Society, 1910, 134.   Similar wooden clappers, semantra, were introduced into the Greek Church; see Neale, Hist. of the Holy East. Ch., 1, 217 et seq., with illustrations.

[5] The Syriac equivalent of the Greek 'salvation.'

people were gathering to the Patriarchal monastery to derive bene-
fits from it,—the Christians of the Faith were not congregating
there, even as they were excused by the Reverend Catholicus, so
that he might meet their [the others'] requirements.[6]

But when this providence which we have recorded had lasted
for a little while, God, the Lord of All, the Lord of death and
departure, took away King Arghon to the Chamber of Delights
and to the Bosom of Abraham.   And upon his removal mourning
oppressed the whole Church under heaven, because those things
which before his time [89*] had been made and then were ruined
were greatly restored.   And who does not suffer greatly from a
change of reign?   For why not, since it is a hard thing and bitter
to speak of, when one knows the nobles and all the royal courtiers,
not to speak of the contemporary king himself?[7]

[KING KAIKATHO AND MAR YABALLAHA]

And when the Church had been in these circumstances for some
time, all at once there arose the younger brother of the deceased
King, one called Irnagin Tongin; and he was crowned as King
Kaikatho, and he took the royal sceptre and sat on his brother's
throne.   And he became King [90*] in 1602 of the Greek Era in
the month Ab.[1]   And the creation was at peace and chaos fled
and hid itself, and the light of righteousness arose and was revealed,
in that the blessed Kaikatho strayed not from the path of his
ancestors.   He confirmed all the religious sectaries each in his
status and honored all the chief dogmas, whether of Christians
or Arabs or Jews or Pagans, and showed partiality to none.   And
he did not waver nor decline from righteousness, gold being con-

---

[6] The text of this period is obscure.

[7] A pertinent complaint against the uncertainties induced by a change of kings
among the Mongols. Arghon died March 10, 1291; see Yule, 1, 36. Subsequent to
his death was the arrival of Marco Polo and his company bringing a bride to him
from the Great Khan, see Int., § ii, end.

[1] I.e., August. According to Bar Hebræus, Chr. syr., p. 578 (Bruns, tr. p. 627),
on Heziran (June) 29, 1603. The author's dating in August may be taken from
the event recorded below. The year is 1291, and Yule gives as the exact date July
23, l. c. Bar Hebræus spells the names 'Kaigathu' and 'Ernagin Turgi.' For the
former Polo writes 'Quiacato,' Prologue, c. 18. According to Bar Hebræus he was
in charge of an army on the Greek marches at his brother's death.

sidered as dung in his eyes, and there was no limit to his alms nor
end to his gifts, for everyone who asked of him received, as is said,
'He who seeks finds' (Matt. 7, 8).[2]   And this truly was in the
way of a [divine] trial.[3]   For when he came to ascend the throne
in the aforesaid month of the year, on the day of the Feast of the
Memorial of the Holy Lady Mary [4]—her prayer be for the world—
in the middle of the month Ab, he entered the church which had
been founded by [91*] Tawos Kathon [4a] in the blessed Camp—and
they [the Court] were then in the mountain called Alatak [5]—while
our father the Catholicus was celebrating the Mysteries.   And
the king was very glad and rejoiced, and he gave the Catholicus
gifts, 20,000 dinars and nine brocaded vestments [6] of first quality.
And there were assembled on that day the sons of the king and
the daughters of the queens and the commanders and magnates,
as well as the forces.   And the praise of the Holy Catholic Church
increased as at the first and even more.   And the mind of the
Christians grew bold, and they were strengthened, knowing the
mind of the Victorious King and hearing his words and attaining
with their hands his gifts and favors.   And day by day their
praise increased and the glory of their Church grew.   And this came
by the great diligence and good management of Mar Yaballaha and
his skill in adulation of the royal household.[7]

[92*] Rabban Sauma then, for he was already growing old
and was weary of the hard discipline of the Mongols and of the life
in the field, received commission from the Victorious King Kaikatho
to build a church in the city of Maragha and to place in it the
ritual equipment of the church which the deceased King Arghon

[2] Bar Hebraeus gives him a totally different character, as one wholly addicted to
sensual pleasures; and so also the Armenian Chronicler, Haithon, see Mosheim, p. 81.

[3] Literally 'in a trial'; presumably the present prosperity of the Church was part
of the divine trial which had another phase in the subsequent political troubles.

[4] On August 15, the Latin Feast of the Assumption.

[4a] The Christian wife of Abaga, see Int. § ii. We learn here for the first time
of her influence in founding the Camp Church.

[5] The Alatak pastures east of Lake Van, where Arghon had built a great summer
palace in the midst of a hunting preserve; see Le Strange, *Eastern Caliphate*, 183,
and his *Nuzhat al-Qulub*, 100.

[6] *Dîbâgê*, a Persian-Arabic word.

[7] This artless statement is a confession of the moral weakness which affected the
statecraft of the Oriental Church in its expansion.   The same weakness appears in its
Chinese missions.

had established in the Camp. And his request was honored by the King. And having received the King's permission, at once he went off with the ritual equipment of the Reverend Catholicus to the city of Maragha. And he founded and built a beautiful church in the name of Mar Mari [8] and the glorious Martyr Mar George.[9] And there were placed in it relics of the Forty Martyrs [10] and of Mar Stephen and of Mar Jacob the Dismembered [11] and also of the martyr Demetrios.[12] And he furnished it with all the finest of ritual equipment. And he obtained the endowments for it, by which the support of its requirements could be maintained, through the help of the glorious Mar Yaballaha [93*] the Catholicus. And in the summer of the next year the Victorious King Kaikatho came twice to the monastery in Maragha and stayed with Mar Catholicus three days. And he rejoiced with very great joy, and he presented and gave great gifts to Mar Catholicus, a *paiza* of gold, that is, a tablet, which was called *sunqor*,[13] and 7000 dinars.

[THE DEATH OF RABBAN SAUMA AND OF THE KINGS KAIKATHO AND BAIDU]

Rabban Sauma was working day and night at this church he was building, and he was transporting the things for it. The amount of the expense put upon that church and of the endowment,

[8] For Mari the Apostle of Iraq see note at p. 22*.

[9] George the Cappadocian, who suffered under Diocletian, A.D. 320, one of the most distinguished of Oriental saints, whose fame travelled Westward. He is known to the Arabs as al-Khidr, and his figure has incorporated many an ancient myth. The two oldest Arabic Christian inscriptions are in churches dedicated to him in the Hauran. See *Dict. Christ. Biog.*, 2, 645, for this saint and the confusion and controversy that have arisen over his name.

[10] There are three sets of Forty Martyrs given by Salmond in *D.C.B.*, 2, 556: those of Sebaste in Armenia, whose Acts are found in the Syriac (Baumstark, *Gesch. d. syr. Lit.*, 93); the Forty of Persia; and 40 Syrian Virgins. Cheikho also notes Forty Martyrs of Sinai. The cult of the Forty was widespread in the East.

[11] The Acts of this martyr (a disciple of Eugenius?) are referred to in lists; see Cureton-Wright, *Anc. Syr. Documents*, 149 *et seq.*, Hoffmann, p. 4.

[12] See *D. C. B.*, 1, 804.

[13] *Sunqor* is Mongolian for 'gerfalcon.' The reference is to the custom described by Polo, iii, c. 7, at Kublai's court: "to certain very great lords also there is given a tablet with gerfalcons on it." Yule in his note, p. 317, knows of no other allusion to such tablets with the gerfalcon device, and so the present statement corroborates Polo.

that is the *waqf* [1] applied to it, was [94*] 105,000 *zûz* more or less.
And he was faithful in his service and prayer, and diligent in constantly offering the Offering, which he instituted in the church.
And he had great satisfaction in the monastery alongside of the
church he had planted. And its embellishment continues until
the present, and constant in it are the services and the Offerings.
May Our Lord render to him the wage of his labor, the delight of
the Heavenly Kingdom, and a portion with the Saints in the
heights above.

And when he had finished the church we have mentioned, he
went down in the service of Mar Catholicus to Baghdad in the year
1605 of the Greek Era [A.D. 1293]. And in the First Tishri [October]
of that year King Baidu,[2] the son of the brother of King Abaga,
made a great feast at a place called Sirzor [3] [95*] on account of the
Catholicus. And he assembled to the banquet his royal family
['sons of his kingdom']. And Rabban Sauma got up from the
feast, his health [4] being undermined, and he fell down seized with a
fever. And on the next day he went off from King Baidu ['Baidar'],
and he reached the city of Arbel, [where he stayed] in the settlement
of necessary affairs and in the pleasure he had with the members
of the church. And Rabban Sauma's illness was increasing, and
he was in distress. And he held out until the Catholicus reached
Baghdad. And the illness increased, and health fled and hope of
life was cut off. And he departed from this world of vanity and
vexation to the world of the Holies and to the city of the Saints,
Jerusalem in Heaven, in the night of the Sunday after Epiphany,
the anthem for which is 'To Thy Church first,' on the tenth of
Kanon [5] of that year. And his body was buried in the Court of
the Romans on the north side of the altar outside in the inner
court, at the south side of [96*] that house of prayer.[6] His portion

---

[1] The usual Arabic word for 'endowment.'

[2] Text, 'Baidar'; of this prince, with the courtesy title of King, more anon.

[3] Probably Shahrazur in western Kurdistan (Bedjan); see Le Strange, *Eastern
Caliphate*, 190.

[4] 'Mixture'; *i.e.*, of the four temperaments constituting the physique.

[5] First Kanon is December, Second Kanon January.

[6] *I.e.*, the grave lay between the church and an altar in the court. This Court
(*dârthâ*) of the Romans is evidently the great monastic compound in Baghdad known
in the Arabic as Dêr er-Rûm; see Le Strange, *Baghdad*, 208 *et seq*. We must interpret

be with the fathers the Catholici, among whom he is placed! And Our Lord rest him, and set him at His right hand in the great day of recompense, when He requites each according to his work by the balance of righteousness and the scales of truth!

And Mar Yaballaha the Catholicus suffered great affliction at his death; and the lamentation reached even to heaven. And he conducted services for the people, not to say in private as well. The magnates, the prefects, that is, the officials, and all the fathers of the city of Baghdad came to comfort him. And hardly did he allow himself comfort on the third day. And he returned to his throne [i.e., to his function]. And it was right for him to feel so, and the law of nature commanded it. For the departed one was strong and effective ['son of arm'] and a help in the office of the patriarchal monastery, not only for Mar Catholicus but for all Christians who gathered to him.

And when the Catholicus had completed that winter in Baghdad, [97*] on the day of the Great Feast [7] he went off to the Camp of the Victorious King Kaikatho in Alatak. He reached the King's Camp, and the latter honored him with many gifts, giving him a fleece garment and two fine mules and assigning him a *sukur*, that is, a *shâthêr*,[8] and presenting him with 60,000 *zûz*. In fine, anything that Mar Catholicus opened his mouth about and desired he did not refuse. And then he returned from the Victorious King. And he laid the foundations of the holy monastery of Mar John Baptist to the north of the city of Maragha at a third of a parasang's distance from it more or less, in that same year at the end of the month Haziran [June], and he raised the walls nearly to completion and its naves to the eaves of the peak.

And all at once the storms arose and waves of chaos were violent in the kingdom. And the emirs were disloyal [98*] to the Kings, and tempests of sufferings prevailed over the world, and commotion fell upon the creation. And men were killed without desert, and many cities were taken with violence by the armies.

the confused story to the effect that the sick man accompanied the Catholicus' party to Baghdad, where he died. The next sentence indicates that this was the burial place of the Patriarchs.

[7] Easter, generally known in the calendar as 'the Sunday of Sundays.'

[8] See note to p. 36*.

And in the winter of 1606 of the Greek Era [A.D. 1295] the roads being cut between Adharbaijan and Baghdad and Diarbekr, the nobles did not cease from the contentions they stirred up, until at last they destroyed King Kaikatho by violence and handed over the kingdom to King Baidu. And this wretched man took it for fear of his life, and he remained on the throne from the 24th Nisan to the 25th Elul [April—September] of that year more or less. And he ruled and reigned in disturbance, and spent his days in fearfulness. And the wiles in those five months and the frauds and mutual [?] tricks between him and the Victorious King Kazan, son of the departed King Arghon, and the stratagems practised by enemies, speech is not now able to encompass, [99*] lest we make the story too long, and the history which is desired turn into something else. To sum up, the murderers of that blessed King Kaikatho contrived the murder of this other King Baidu. And there befell division, and civilization was disturbed, and the hordes of the Arabs roused up to avenge themselves upon the Church and her children for their losses through the father of those Kings. Then suddenly on the Sunday 'The mouth cannot,' in that same year, on the 25th Elul of the aforesaid year, there was heard the rumor of the flight of King Baidu and of his destruction, and with it came trials, which in truth were by the permission of God.[9]

---

[9] The above agitated picture of the breaking of the Muslim storm upon the Church is filled out by the facts of history. Kaikatho was done away with by a conspiracy, his cousin Baidu raised to a troubled throne and a brief reign of eight months. Although inclined most friendly to the Christians he had to confess Islam. But the Muslims, not satisfied, offered the throne to a son of Arghon, Ghazan, on condition that he should whole-heartedly accept their cause. The latter attacked Baidu in the field, killed him, and gained the crown. But the new king still favored the Christians and is reputed to have permitted their religion in his own family. But he was not strong enough to restrain the murderous attacks of the Muslims against the Christians, and the rest of this Biography gives the ugly picture of the internecine strife between the two religions, which ended in the collapse of the Christians. It was this Kazan ('Casan') who married the Chinese lady from Kublai's court who was sent in charge of Marco Polo as a bride for his father Arghon, and who arrived after the latter's death. For this subsequent history see the end of Bar Hebræus, *Chron. syr.*, and his *Chron. eccles.*, cited in Assemani, iii, part ii, c. 7, and the capital survey in Mosheim, pp. 82 *et seq.*

INDEX

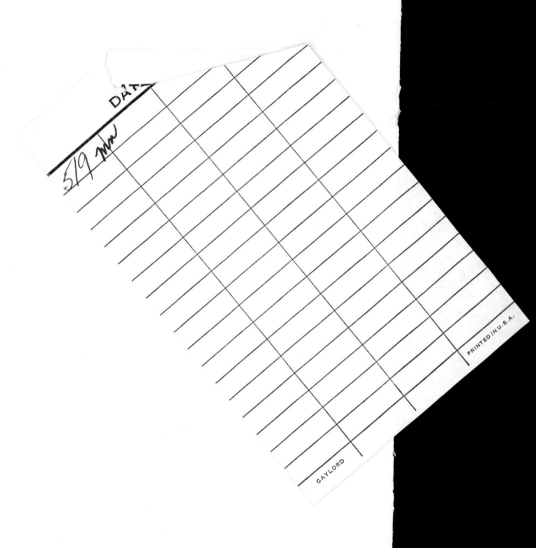

DATE

5/9 mm

GAYLORD

PRINTED IN U.S.A.